# *The Way to*
# HAPPINESS

## A COMMON SENSE GUIDE TO BETTER LIVING

*FOR MORE INFORMATION*
CALL DENNIS AT 408-390-8431

*To:* _____

*From:* _____

# The Way to
# HAPPINESS

THE WAY TO HAPPINESS FOUNDATION

Published by The Way to Happiness Foundation International

ISBN 978-1-59970-053-3

Printed in the United States of America

# CONTENTS

# HOW TO USE
# THIS BOOK

*Y*ou of course
wish to help your contacts
and friends.

Choose someone
whose actions, however remotely,
may influence your own survival.

Write the person's name
on the top line
of the front page of this book.

Write or stamp your own name,
as an individual, on the second line.

Present the person with the book.

Ask the person to read it.[0]

You will find that he or she also
is threatened with the
possible misconduct of others.

0. Words sometimes have several different meanings. The footnote definitions given in this book only give the meaning of the word as it is used in the text. If you find any words in this book you do not know, look them up in a good dictionary. If you do not, then misunderstandings and possible arguments can arise.

Give the person several
additional copies of this book
but do not write your name on them:
let the other person write his or hers.
Have the person present these copies
to others that are involved in
his or her life.

By continuing to do this
you will greatly enhance your own
survival potential and theirs.

*This is a way toward a much safer
and happier life for you and others.*

# WHY I GAVE YOU
# THIS BOOK

$\mathcal{Y}$our

survival[1]

is

important

to

me.

---

1. *survival:* the act of remaining alive, of continuing to exist, of being alive.

# HAPPINESS[2]

$\mathcal{T}$rue joy
and happiness are valuable.

If one does not survive,
no joy and no happiness are obtainable.

Trying to survive in a chaotic,[3] dishonest
and generally immoral[4] society is difficult.

Any individual or group seeks
to obtain from life what pleasure
and freedom from pain
that they can.

2. *happiness:* a condition or state of well-being, contentment, pleasure; joyful, cheerful, untroubled existence; the reaction to having nice things happen to one.
3. *chaotic:* having the character or nature of total disorder or confusion.
4. *immoral:* not moral; not following good practices of behavior; not doing right; lacking any idea of proper conduct.

Your own survival can be threatened
by the bad actions of others around you.

Your own happiness can be turned to
tragedy and sorrow by the dishonesty
and misconduct of others.

I am sure you can think of
instances of this actually happening.
Such wrongs reduce one's survival
and impair one's happiness.

You are important to other people.
You are listened to.
You can influence others.

The happiness or unhappiness
of others you could name
is important to you.

Without too much trouble,
using this book,
you can help them survive
and lead happier lives.

While no one can guarantee
that anyone else can be happy,
their chances of survival
and happiness can be improved.
And with theirs, yours will be.

*It is in your power to point the way
to a less dangerous and happier life.*

# 1.

# TAKE CARE OF YOURSELF.

## 1-1.
### *Get care when you are ill.*

When they are ill,
even with communicable diseases, people often
do not isolate themselves or seek proper treatment.
This, as you can easily see, tends to put you at risk.
Insist when someone is ill that he or she takes
the proper precautions and gets proper care.

## 1-2.
### *Keep your body clean.*

People who do not bathe or wash
their hands regularly, can carry germs.
They put you at risk. You are well within
your rights to insist that people bathe regularly
and wash their hands. It is inevitable that
one gets dirty working or exercising.
Get them to clean up afterwards.

## 1-3.
### *Preserve your teeth.*

If one brushed one's teeth
after every meal, it has been said that
one would not suffer tooth decay.
This, or chewing gum after each meal,
goes far toward defending others
from oral diseases and bad breath.
Suggest to others that
they preserve their teeth.

## 1-4.
### *Eat properly.*

People who do not eat properly are not
of much help to you or themselves.
They tend to have a low energy level.
They are sometimes ill-tempered.
They become ill more easily.
It doesn't require strange diets
to eat properly but it does require
that one eats nourishing
food regularly.

# 1-5.

## *Get rest.*

Although many times in life one has to
work beyond normal sleep periods,
a person's general failure to get proper rest
can make him or her a burden to others.
Tired people are not alert. They can make mistakes.
They have accidents. Just when you need them
they can dump the whole workload on one.
They put others at risk. Insist that people
who do not get proper rest do so.

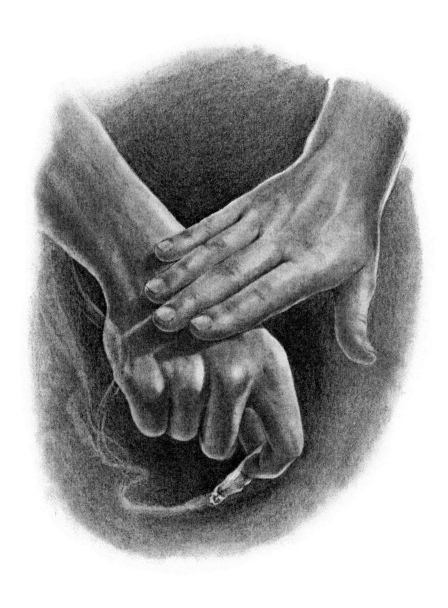

# 2.

## BE TEMPERATE.[5]

### 2-1.
### *Do not take harmful drugs.*

People who take drugs
do not always see the real world
in front of them. They are not really *there*.
On a highway, in casual contact, in a home,
they can be very dangerous to you.
People mistakenly believe they
"feel better" or "act better" or are
"only happy" when on drugs.
This is just another delusion.
Sooner or later the drugs
will destroy them physically.
Discourage people from taking drugs.
When they are doing so, encourage them
to seek help in getting off of them.

---

5. *temperate:* not going to extremes; not overdoing things; controlling one's cravings.

# 2-2.

## *Do not take alcohol to excess.*

People who take alcohol are not alert.
It impairs their ability to react
even when it seems to them
they are more alert because of it.
Alcohol has some medicinal value.
It can be grossly overestimated.
Don't let anyone who has been drinking
drive you in a car or fly you in a plane.
Drinking can take lives in more ways than one.
A little liquor goes a long way; don't let
too much of it wind up in unhappiness or death.
Deter[6] people from excessive drinking.

*Observing the points above,*
*one becomes more physically able to enjoy life.*

---

6. *deter:* to prevent or discourage.

# 3.

# DON'T BE
# PROMISCUOUS.[7]

$S$ex is the means
by which the race projects itself into
the future through children and the family.
A lot of pleasure and happiness can come from sex:
nature intended it that way so the race would go on.
But, misused or abused, it carries with it
heavy penalties and punishments:
nature seems to have intended it
that way also.

7. *promiscuous:* casual, random sexual relations.

## 3-1.

# *Be faithful to your sexual partner.*

Unfaithfulness on
the part of a sexual partner
can heavily reduce one's survival.
History and the newspapers carry floods
of instances of the violence of human passions
aroused by unfaithfulness. "Guilt" is the milder evil.
Jealousy and vengeance are the greater monsters:
one never knows when they will cease to sleep.
It is all very well to speak of "being civilized"
and "uninhibited" and "understanding";
no talk will mend ruined lives.
A "feeling of guilt" is nowhere near
as sharp as a knife in the back
or ground glass in the soup.

Additionally, there is the question of health.
If you do not insist upon faithfulness from a
sexual partner, you lay yourself open to disease.
For a very brief period, it was said that
sexual diseases were all under control.
This is not now the case, if it ever was.
Incurable strains of such diseases now exist.

The problems of sexual misbehavior are not new.
The powerful religion of Buddhism in India
vanished from there in the seventh century.
According to its own historians, the cause
was sexual promiscuity in its monasteries.
More modernly, when sexual promiscuity
becomes prevalent in an organization,
commercial or otherwise, the organization
can be seen to fail. No matter how
civilized their discussions about it,
families shatter in the face
of unfaithfulness.

The urge of the moment
can become the sorrow of a lifetime.
Impress those around you with that
and safeguard your own health and pleasure.

*Sex is a big step on the way to happiness and joy.*
*There is nothing wrong with it if it is followed*
*with faithfulness and decency.*

# 4.

# LOVE AND HELP
# CHILDREN.

*T*oday's children
will become tomorrow's civilization.
Bringing a child into the world today is
a little bit like dropping one into a tiger's cage.
Children can't handle their environment[8]
and they have no real resources.
They need love and help
to make it.

8. *environment:* one's surroundings; the material things around one; the area one lives in; the living things, objects, spaces and forces with which one lives whether close to or far away.

It is a delicate problem to discuss.
There are almost as many theories on how to
raise a child or not raise him as there are parents.
Yet if one does it wrong much grief can result and
one may even complicate his or her own later years.
Some try to raise children the way they were
themselves raised, others attempt the exact
opposite, many hold to an idea that children
should just be let grow on their own.
None of these guarantee success.
The last method is based on a materialistic[9] idea
that the development of the child parallels
the evolutionary[10] history of the race;
that in some magical way, unexplained,
the "nerves" of the child will "ripen" as
he or she grows older and the result will be a
moral,[11] well-behaving adult. Although the theory
is disproven with ease—simply by noticing the
large criminal population whose nerves somehow
did not ripen—it is a lazy way to raise children and
achieves some popularity. It doesn't take care of
your civilization's future or your older years.

9. *materialistic:* the opinion that only physical matter exists.
10. *evolutionary:* related to a very ancient theory that all plants and animals developed from simpler forms and were shaped by their surroundings rather than being planned or created.
11. *moral:* able to know right from wrong in conduct; deciding and acting from that understanding.

A child is a little bit like a blank slate.
If you write the wrong things on it,
it will say the wrong things.
But, unlike a slate, a child can begin
to do the writing: the child tends to write
what has been written already.
The problem is complicated by the fact that,
while most children are capable of great
decency, a few are born insane and, today,
some are even born as drug addicts:
but such cases are an unusual few.

It does no good just to try to "buy" the child
with an overwhelm of toys and possessions
or to smother and protect the child:
the result can be pretty awful.

One has to make up his mind what he is
trying to get the child to become:
this is modified by several things:
(a) what the child basically *can* become
due to inherent make-up and potential;
(b) what the child really wants to become;
(c) what one wants the child to become;
(d) the resources available. But remember that
whatever these all add up to, the child will *not*
survive well unless he or she eventually
becomes self-reliant and *very* moral.
Otherwise the end product is likely to be
a liability to everyone including the child.

Whatever one's affection for the child,
remember that the child cannot survive well
in the long run if he or she does not have
his or her feet put on the way to survival.
It will be no accident if the child goes wrong:
the contemporary society is tailor-made
for a child's failure.

It will help enormously if you obtain a child's
understanding of and agreement to follow
the precepts[12] contained in this book.

What does have a workability is simply to
try to be the child's friend. It is certainly true
that a child needs friends. Try to find out what
a child's problem really is and, without crushing
their own solutions, try to help solve them.
Observe them—and this applies even to babies.
Listen to what children tell you about their lives.
Let *them* help—if you don't, they become
overwhelmed with a sense of obligation[13]
which they then must repress.

12. *precepts:* rules or statements advising or laying down a principle or
principles or a course of action regarding conduct; directions meant as a rule
or rules for conduct.
13. *obligation:* the condition or fact of owing another something in return for
things, favors or services received.

It will help the child
enormously if you obtain
understanding of and agreement
to this way to happiness
and get him or her to follow it.
It could have an enormous effect
on the child's survival—and yours.

A child factually does not
do well without love.
Most children have an
abundance of it to return.

*The way to happiness
has on its route the loving and
the helping of children from babyhood
to the brink of adult life.*

# 5.

# HONOR[14] AND HELP YOUR PARENTS.

*F*rom a child's
point of view, parents are sometimes
hard to understand.

There are differences between generations.
But truthfully, this is no barrier.
When one is weak, it is a temptation
to take refuge in subterfuges and lies:
it is this which builds the wall.

14. *honor:* to show respect for; to treat with deference and courtesy.

Children *can* reconcile their
differences with their parents.
Before any shouting begins, one can
at least try to talk it over quietly.
If the child is frank and honest,
there cannot help but be an appeal
that will reach. It is often possible to
attain a compromise[15] where both sides
now understand and can agree.
It is not always easy to
get along with others
but one should try.

One cannot overlook the fact
that almost always, parents are acting from
a very strong desire to do what they believe
to be best for the child.

15. *compromise:* a settlement of differences in which each side gives in on
some point while retaining others and reaching a mutual agreement thereby.

Children are indebted to their parents
for their upbringing—if the parents did so.
While some parents are so fiercely independent
that they will accept no return on the obligation,
it is nevertheless true that there often comes
a time when it is the turn of the younger
generation to care for their parents.

In spite of all, one must remember that
they are the only parents one has.
And as such, no matter what,
one should honor them
and help them.

*The way to happiness includes
being on good terms with one's parents
or those who brought one up.*

# 6.

# SET A
# GOOD EXAMPLE.[16]

*T*here are many people
one influences.[17] The influence[18] can be
good or it can be bad.

If one conducts his life
to keep these recommendations,
one is setting a good example.

Others around one cannot help
but be influenced by this,
no matter what they say.

16. *example:* someone or something worthy of imitation or duplication;
a pattern, a model.
17. *influences:* has an effect upon.
18. *influence:* the resulting effect.

Anyone trying to discourage you
is trying to do so because they factually
mean you harm or are seeking
to serve their own ends.
Down deep, they will respect you.

Your own survival chances will be bettered
in the long run since others, influenced,
will become less of a threat.
There are other benefits.

Don't discount the effect you can achieve
on others simply by mentioning these
things and setting a good example
in your own right.

*The way to happiness requires that one
set a good example for others.*

# 7.

## SEEK TO LIVE
## WITH THE TRUTH.[19]

*F*alse data can
cause one to make stupid mistakes.
It can even block one from
absorbing true data.

One can solve the problems of existence
only when he has true data.

If those around one lie to him or her,
one is led into making errors and
his survival potential is reduced.

19. *truth:* that which agrees with the facts and observations; logical answers
resulting from looking over all the facts and data; a conclusion based on
evidence uninfluenced by desire, authority or prejudice; an inevitable
(unavoidable) fact no matter how arrived at.

False data can come from many sources:
academic, social, professional.

Many want you to believe things
just to suit their own ends.

What is *true* is what is true for *you.*

No one has any right to force data off on you
and command you to believe it or else.
If it is not true for you, it isn't true.

Think your own way through things,
accept what is true for you, discard the rest.
There is nothing unhappier than one
who tries to live in a chaos of lies.

## 7-1.

# $D$o not tell harmful lies.[20]

Harmful lies are
the product of fear, malice and envy.
They can drive people to acts of desperation.
They can ruin lives. They create a kind of trap
into which the teller and the target can both fall.
Interpersonal and social chaos can result.
Many wars began because of harmful lies.

One should learn to detect them
and reject them.

## 7-2.

# $D$o not bear false witness.

There are considerable penalties
connected with swearing or testifying to
untrue "facts"; it is called "perjury":
it has heavy penalties.

*The way to happiness*
*lies along the road to truth.*

---

20. *lies:* false statements or pieces of information deliberately presented as
being true; a falsehood; anything meant to deceive or give a wrong impression.

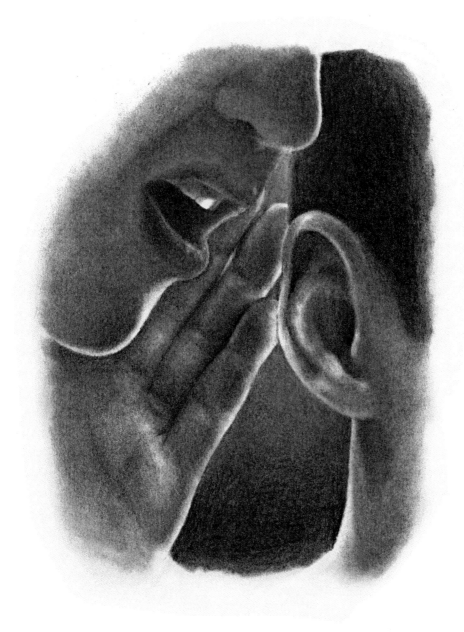

# 8.

# DO NOT MURDER.[21]

*M*ost races,
from the most ancient times to the present,
have prohibited murder and punished it heavily.
Sometimes this has been broadened to say,
"Thou shalt not kill," when a later translation
of the same work has found it to read
"Thou shalt not murder."

There is a considerable difference
between these two words "kill" and "murder."
A prohibition against all killing would rule out
self-defense; it would tend to make it illegal
to handle a serpent coiling to strike the baby;
it would put a race on a diet of vegetables.
I am sure you can see many illustrations of
the difficulties raised by a prohibition
against all killing.

---

21. *murder:* the unlawful killing of one (or more) human being by another, especially with malice aforethought (intending to do so before the act).

"Murder" is another thing entirely.
By definition it means, "The unlawful killing
of one (or more) human being by another,
especially with malice aforethought."
One can easily see that in this age of violent
weaponry, murder would be all too easy.
One could not exist in a society where
oneself or one's family or friends
were at the mercy of some who
went about casually taking lives.

Murder justly bears the highest priority
in social prevention and retaliation.

The stupid, the evil and the insane seek to
solve their real or imagined problems with murder.
And they have been known to do it
for no reason at all.

Get behind any demonstratedly effective program
that handles this threat to Mankind and push.
Your own survival could depend upon it.

*The way to happiness does not include murdering
or your friends, your family or yourself
being murdered.*

# 9.

# DON'T DO ANYTHING ILLEGAL.

*"I*llegal acts"
are those which are prohibited by
official rules or law. They are the product
of rulers, legislative bodies and judges.
They are usually written down in law codes.
In a well-ordered society, these are
published and made known generally.
In a cloudy—and often crime-ridden—society
one has to consult an attorney or be
specially trained to know them all:
such a society will tell one that
"ignorance is no excuse for
breaking the law."

Any member of society, however,
has a responsibility, whether young or old,
for knowing what that society considers to be
an "illegal act." People can be asked,
libraries exist where they can be looked up.

An "illegal act" is not disobedience
to some casual order like "go to bed."
It is an action, which if done, can result in
punishment by the courts and state—being
pilloried[22] by the state propaganda[23] machine,
fines and even imprisonment.

When one does something illegal, small or large,
one is laid open to an attack by the state.
It does not matter whether one is caught
or not, when one does an illegal act,
one has weakened one's defenses.

Almost any worthwhile thing
one is trying to accomplish
often can be done in perfectly legal ways.

22. *pilloried:* exposed to ridicule, public contempt, scorn or abuse.
23. *propaganda:* spreading ideas, information or rumor to further one's own
cause and/or injure that of another, often without regard to truth; the act
of putting lies in the press or on radio and TV so that when a person comes to
trial he will be found guilty; the action of falsely damaging a person's reputation
so he will not be listened to. (A propagandist is a person or group that does,
makes or practices propaganda.)

The "illegal" route
is a dangerous and time-wasting shortcut.
Imagined "advantages" in committing illegal acts
usually turn out not to be worth it.

The state and government tends to be
a rather unthinking machine. It exists and works
on laws and codes of laws. It is geared to
strike down through its channels at illegality.
As such it can be an implacable[24] enemy,
adamant[25] on the subject of "illegal acts."
The rightness and wrongness of things do not
count in the face of laws and codes of laws.
Only the laws count.

When you realize or discover that those about you
are committing "illegal acts," you should
do what you can to discourage it. You yourself,
not even a party to it, can yet suffer because of it.
The firm's accountant falsifies the books:
in any resulting commotion,
the firm could fail and you could lose your job.
Such instances can grossly affect one's own survival.

24. *implacable:* not open to being quieted, soothed or pleased; remorseless; relentless.
25. *adamant:* hard; not giving in; unyielding; something which won't break; insistent; refusing any other opinion; surrendering to nothing.

As a member of any group subject to laws,
encourage the clear-cut publication of those laws so
they can be known. Support any legal political effort
to reduce, clarify and codify the laws
that apply to that group. Adhere to
the principle that all men are equal under law,
a principle which, in its own time
and place—the tyrannical[26] days of aristocracy[27]—was
one of the greatest social advances in human history
and should not be lost sight of.

See that children and people become
informed of what is "legal" and what is "illegal"
and make it known, if by as little as a frown,
that you do not approve of "illegal acts."

Those who commit them, even when they
"get away with them," are yet weakened
before the might of the state.

*The way to happiness
does not include the fear of being found out.*

26. *tyrannical:* the use of cruel, unjust and absolute power; crushing;
oppressing; harsh; severe.
27. *aristocracy:* government by a few with special privileges, ranks or
positions; rule by an elite few who are above the general law; a group who by
birth or position are "superior to everybody else" and who can make or apply
laws to others but consider they themselves are not affected by the laws.

# 10.

## SUPPORT A GOVERNMENT DESIGNED AND RUN FOR ALL THE PEOPLE.

*U*nscrupulous and
evil men and groups can usurp the power
of government and use it to their own ends.

Government organized and conducted solely for
self-interested individuals and groups
gives the society a short life span.
This imperils the survival of everyone in the land;
it even imperils those who attempt it.
History is full of such governmental deaths.

Opposition to
such governments usually
just brings on more violence.

But one can
raise his voice in caution
when such abuses are abroad.
And one need not actively
support such a government;
doing nothing illegal, it is yet possible,
by simply withdrawing one's cooperation,
to bring about an eventual reform.
Even as this is being written, there are
several governments in the world
that are failing only because their people
express their silent disagreement
by simply not cooperating.
These governments are at risk:
any untimely wind of mischance
could blow them over.

On the other hand,
where a government is obviously working hard
for ALL its people, rather than for some
special interest group or insane dictator,
one should support it to the limit.

There is a subject called "government."
In schools, they mostly teach "civics"
which is merely how the
current organization is put together.
The real subject, "government"
goes under various headings:
political economy, political philosophy,
political power, etc. The whole subject of
"government" and how to govern can be
quite precise, almost a technical science.
If one is interested in having a better government,
one that does not cause trouble, one should
suggest it be taught at earlier ages in schools;
one can also read up on it:
it is not a very difficult subject
if you look up the big words.

It is, after all,
the people and their own opinion leaders
who sweat and fight and bleed for their country.
A government cannot bleed, it cannot even smile:
it is just an idea men have.
It is the individual person who is alive — *you.*

*The way to happiness
is hard to travel
when shadowed with
the oppression of tyranny.
A benign government,
designed and run for ALL the people,
has been known to smooth the way:
when such occurs, it deserves support.*

# 11.

## DO NOT HARM A PERSON OF GOOD WILL.[28]

*D*espite the insistence
of evil men that all men are evil, there are
many good men around and women too.
You may have been fortunate enough
to know some.

Factually, the society runs
on men and women of good will.
Public workers, opinion leaders, those in
the private sector who do their jobs are,
in the great majority, people of good will.
If they weren't, they long since
would have ceased to serve.

---

28. *will:* bearing or attitude toward others; disposition. Traditionally, "men of good will" means those who mean well toward their fellows and work to help them.

Such people are easy to attack:
their very decency prevents them from
overprotecting themselves. Yet the survival
of most of the individuals in a society
depends upon them.

The violent criminal,
the propagandist, the sensation-seeking media
all tend to distract one's attention from
the solid, everyday fact that the society would
not run at all were it not for the individuals
of good will. As they guard the street,
counsel the children, take the temperatures,
put out the fires and speak good sense
in quiet voices, one is apt to overlook the fact
that people of good will are the ones that
keep the world going and Man alive
upon this Earth.

Yet such can be attacked and
strong measures should be advocated
and taken to defend them and keep them
from harm, for your own survival
and that of your family and friends
depends upon them.

*The way to happiness*
*is far more easily followed when one*
*supports people of good will.*

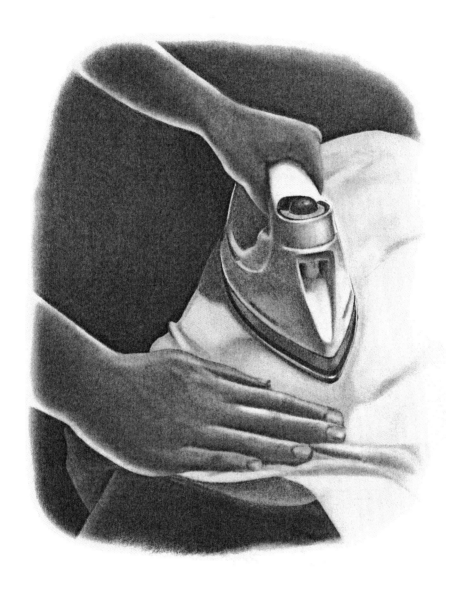

# 12.

# SAFEGUARD[29] AND IMPROVE YOUR ENVIRONMENT.

## 12-1.

## *Be of good appearance.*

It sometimes does not occur to
some individuals—as they do not have to
spend their days looking at themselves—that
they form part of the scenery and appearance
of others. And some do not realize
that they are judged by others
on the basis of their appearance.

While clothes can be expensive,
soap and the other tools of self-care
are not that hard to obtain.
The techniques are sometimes
difficult to dig up but can be evolved.

29. *safeguard:* prevent from being harmed; protect.

In some societies, when they are
barbaric or become very degraded,
it can even be the fashion to be a public eyesore.
Actually it is a symptom of a lack of self-respect.

Exercising and working,
one can become very messed up.
But this does not rule out getting cleaned up.
And, as an example, some European
and English workmen manage
a style of appearance even when working.
Some of the better athletes, one notices,
look good despite being wringing wet with sweat.

An environment
disfigured with unkempt people
can have a subtle, depressing effect
on one's morale.[30]

Encourage people around you
to look good by complimenting them
when they do or even gently helping them
with their problems when they don't.
It could improve their self-regard
and their morale as well.

30. *morale:* the mental and emotional attitude of an individual or a group;
sense of well-being; willingness to get on with it; a sense of common purpose.

# 12-2.
## *Take care of your own area.*

When people mess up their own possessions
and area, it can slop over into your own.

When people seem to be incapable of caring
for their own things and places, it is a symptom
of their feeling that they don't really belong there
and don't really own their own things. When young,
the things they were "given" had too many cautions
and strings attached or were taken away from
them by brothers, sisters or parents.
And they possibly did not feel welcome.

The possessions, the rooms and work spaces,
the vehicles of such people
advertise that they are not really
the property of anyone.
Worse, a sort of rage against possessions
can sometimes be seen.
Vandalism[31] is a manifestation of it:
the house or car "nobody owns" is soon ruined.

31. *vandalism:* the willful and malicious destruction of public or private
property, especially anything beautiful or artistic.

Those who build and try to maintain
low-income housing are often dismayed by
the rapidity with which ruin can set in.
The poor, by definition, own little or nothing.
Harassed in various ways, they also come to feel
they do not belong.

But whether rich or poor,
and for whatever reason, people who do not
take care of their possessions and places
can cause disorder to those about them.
I am sure you can think of such instances.

Ask such people what they really do own in life
and if they really belong where they are
and you will receive some surprising answers.
And help them a great deal too.

The skill of organizing
possessions and places
can be taught.
It can come as
a new idea to someone
that an item,
when picked up and used,
should be put back in the same place
so it can be found again:
some spend half their time
just looking for things.
A little time spent getting organized
can pay off in speeded work:
it is not the waste of time some believe.

To protect your own possessions and places,
get others to take care of theirs.

## 12-3.

# *Help take care of the planet.*

The idea that one has a share in the planet and
that one can and should help care for it may seem
very large and, to some, quite beyond reality.
But today what happens on the other side
of the world, even so far away, can effect
what happens in your own home.

Recent discoveries by space probes to Venus
have shown that our own world
could be deteriorated to a point where
it would no longer support life.
And it possibly could happen
in one's own lifetime.

Cut down too many forests,
foul too many rivers and seas,
mess up the atmosphere and we have had it.
The surface temperature can go roasting hot,
the rain can turn to sulfuric acid.
All living things could die.

One can ask,
"Even if that were true,
what could I do about it?"
Well, even if one were simply to frown
when people do things to mess up the planet,
one would be doing something about it.
Even if one only had the opinion that it was
just not a good thing to wreck the planet
and mentioned that opinion,
one would be doing something.

Care of the planet begins in one's own front yard.
It extends through the area one travels
to get to school or work. It covers such places
as where one picnics or goes on vacation.
The litter which messes up the terrain and
water supply, the dead brush which invites fire,
these are things one need not contribute to
and which, in otherwise idle moments,
one can do something about.
Planting a tree may seem little enough
but it is something.

In some countries, old people, the unemployed
do not just sit around and go to pieces:
they are used to care for the gardens
and parks and forests, to pick up the litter
and add some beauty to the world.
There is no lack of resources to take care of
the planet. They are mainly ignored.
One notes that the Civilian Conservation Corps
in the US, organized in the 1930s to absorb
the energies of unemployed officers and youth,
was one of the few, if not the only project
of that depressed era, that created far more
wealth for the state than was expended.
It reforested large areas and did other valuable
things that cared for the US part of the planet.
One notes that the CCC no longer exists.
One can do as little as add one's opinion that such
projects are worthwhile and support opinion
leaders and organizations that carry on
environmental work.

There is no lack of technology.
But technology and its application cost money.
Money is available when sensible economic policies,
policies which do not penalize everyone,
are followed. Such policies exist.

There are many things one can do
to help take care of the planet.
They begin with the idea that one should.
They progress with suggesting
to others they should.

Man has gotten up to the potential of
destroying the planet. He must be pushed on up
to the capability and actions of saving it.

It is, after all, what we're standing on.

*If others do not help safeguard and improve
the environment, the way to happiness could have
no roadbed to travel on at all.*

# 13.

# DO NOT
# STEAL.

*W*hen one does not
respect the ownership of things, his own
possessions and property are at risk.

A person who, for one reason or another,
has been unable to honestly accumulate possessions,
can pretend that nobody owns anything anyway.
But don't try to steal his shoes!

A thief sows the environment with mysteries:
what happened to this, what happened to that?
A thief causes trouble far in excess
of the value of things stolen.

Faced with the advertising of desirable goods,
torn by the incapability of doing anything
valuable enough to acquire possessions
or simply driven by an impulse,
those who steal imagine they are
acquiring something valuable at low cost.
But that is the difficulty: the cost.
The actual price to the thief
is high beyond belief.
The greatest robbers in history
paid for their loot by spending their lives
in wretched hide-outs and prisons
with only rare moments of "the good life."
No amount of stolen valuables
would reward such a horrible fate.

Stolen goods greatly reduce in value:
they have to be hidden, they are always
a threat to liberty itself.

Even in communist states, the thief
is sent to prison.

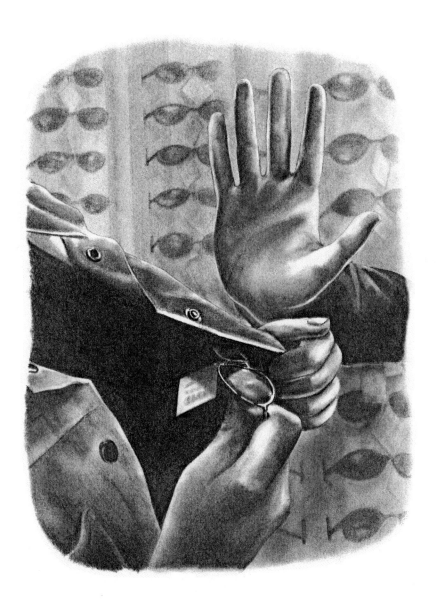

Stealing things is really just
an admission that one is not
capable enough to make it honestly.
Or that one has a streak of insanity.
Ask a thief which one it is:
it's either one or the other.

*The road to happiness cannot be traveled
with stolen goods.*

# 14.

# BE WORTHY
# OF TRUST.

*U*nless
one can have confidence
in the reliability of those about one,
he himself is at risk.
When those he counts upon
let him down, his own life
can become disordered
and even his own survival
can be put at risk.

Mutual trust is
the firmest building block
in human relationships.
Without it, the whole structure
comes down.

Trustworthiness is
a highly esteemed commodity.
When one has it,
one is considered valuable.
When one has lost it,
one may be considered
worthless.

One should
get others around one
to demonstrate it and earn it.
They will become much more valuable
to themselves and others thereby.

## 14-1.

# *Keep your word once given.*

When one gives an assurance or
promise or makes a sworn intention,
one must make it come true.
If one says he is going to do something,
he should do it. If he says he is not going to
do something, he should not do it.

One's regard for another is based,
in no small degree, on whether or not
the person keeps his or her word.
Even parents, for instance, would be surprised
at the extent they drop in the opinion of their
children when a promise is not kept.

People who keep their word are trusted
and admired. People who do not
are regarded like garbage.

Those who break their word
often never get another chance.

A person who does not keep his word
can soon find himself entangled and trapped
in all manner of "guarantees" and "restrictions"
and can even find himself shut off from
normal relations with others.
There is no more thorough self-exile
from one's fellows than to fail to
keep one's promises once made.

One should never permit another to give
his or her word lightly. And one should insist
that when a promise is made, it must be kept.
One's own life can become very disordered in
trying to associate with people who
do not keep their promises.
It is not a casual matter.

*The way to happiness is*
*much, much easier to travel*
*with people one can trust.*

# 15.

# FULFILL YOUR
# OBLIGATIONS.[32]

*I*n going through life,
one inevitably incurs obligations.
Factually, one is born with
certain obligations and they tend
to accumulate thereafter. It is no novel
or new idea that one owes his parents a debt for
bringing one into the world, for raising one.
It is a credit to parents that they don't push it
any harder than they do.
But it is an obligation, nevertheless:
even the child feels it. And as life continues
to run its course, one accumulates
other obligations—to other persons,
to friends, to society and even the world.

---

32. *obligation:* the state, fact or condition of being indebted to another for
a special service or favor received; a duty, contract, promise or any other
social, moral or legal requirement that binds one to follow or avoid a certain
course of action; the sense of owing another.

It is an extreme disservice to a person
not to permit him to satisfy or pay off
his obligations. No small part of
the "revolt of childhood" is caused
by others refusing to accept
the only "coins" a baby or child or youth has
with which to discharge the "weight of obligation":
the baby's smiles, the child's fumbling efforts to help,
the youth's possible advice or
just the effort to be a good son or a good daughter
commonly pass unrecognized, unaccepted;
they can be ill-aimed, often ill-planned;
they fade quickly. Such efforts, when they
fail to discharge the enormity of the debt,
can be replaced with any number of
mechanisms or rationalizations:
"one doesn't really owe anything,"
"I was owed it all in the first place,"
"I didn't ask to be born,"
"my parents or guardians are no good,"
and "life isn't worth living anyway,"
to name a few.
And yet the obligations
continue to pile up.

The "weight of obligation"
can be a crushing burden if one can see
no way to discharge it. It can bring about
all manner of individual or social disorders.
When it cannot be discharged, those who are owed,
often unwittingly, find themselves targets
for the most unlooked-for reactions.

One can help a person who finds himself in the
dilemma of unpaid obligations and debt by simply
going over with him or her *all* the obligations they
have incurred and have not fulfilled—moral,
social and financial—and work out some
way to discharge *all* of those the
person feels are still owed.

One should accept the efforts of a child
or an adult to pay off non-financial obligations
they feel they may owe: one should help
bring about some mutually agreeable solution
to the discharge of financial ones.

Discourage a person from
incurring more obligations than it is
possible for him or her
to actually discharge
or repay.

*The way to happiness*
*is very hard to travel when one*
*is burdened with the weight of*
*obligations which one is owed or*
*which he has not discharged.*

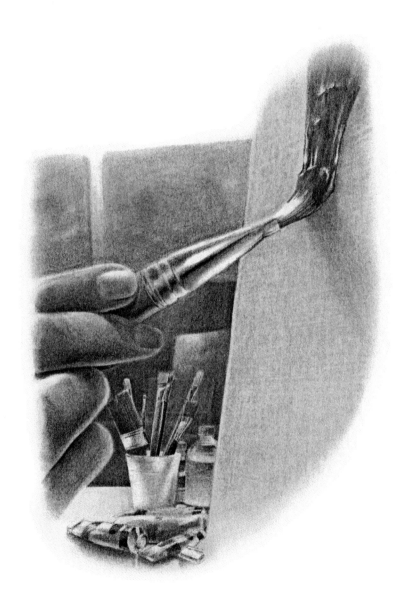

# 16.

# BE INDUSTRIOUS.[33]

*W*ork is
not always pleasant.

But few are unhappier than those who
lead a purposeless, idle and bored existence:
children gloom to their mother when they have
nothing to do; the low-mindedness of the
unemployed, even when they are on "relief"[34]
or the "dole"[35] is legendary; the retired man,
with nothing further to accomplish in life,
perishes from inactivity, as shown
by statistics.

33. *industrious:* applying oneself with energy to study or work; actively and
purposefully getting things done; opposite of being idle and accomplishing
nothing.
34. *relief:* goods or money given by a government agency to people because
of need or poverty.
35. *dole:* the British term for government relief.

Even the tourist, lured by a travel agency's
call to leisure, gives a tour conductor a bad time
if he has nothing for them to do.

Sorrow itself can be eased by
simply getting busy at something.

Morale is boosted to high highs
by accomplishment. In fact, it can be
demonstrated that production[36] is
the basis of morale.

People who are not industrious
dump the workload on those around them.
They tend to burden one.

It is hard to get along with idle people.
Aside from depressing one,
they can also be a bit dangerous.

36. *production:* the act of completing something; finishing a task, project or
object that is useful or valuable or simply worth doing or having.

A workable answer is to persuade such to decide
on some activity and get them busy with it.
The most lasting benefit will be found to arise
from work that leads to actual production.

*The way to happiness is
a high road when it includes industriousness
that leads to tangible production.*

# 17.

# BE
# COMPETENT.[37]

*I*n an age of
intricate equipment and high-speed
machines and vehicles, one's survival
and that of one's family and friends depends
in no small measure upon the
general competence of others.

In the marketplace, in the sciences, the humanities
and in the government, incompetence[38] can
threaten the lives and future of
the few or the many.

37. *competent:* able to do well those things one does; capable; skilled in doing
what one does; measuring up to the demands of one's activities.
38. *incompetence:* lacking adequate knowledge or skill or ability; unskilled;
incapable; subject to making big errors or mistakes; bungling.

I am sure you can think of
many examples of these things.

Man has always had
an impulse to control his fate.
Superstition, propitiation of the right gods,
ritual dances before the hunt,
can all be viewed as efforts,
no matter how faint or unavailing,
to control destiny.

It was not until he learned to think,
to value knowledge and to apply it
with competent skill, that he began to
dominate his environment.
The true "gift of heaven" may have been
the potential to be competent.

In common pursuits and activities,
Man respects skill and ability.
These in a hero or athlete
are almost worshiped.

The test of true competence
is the end result.

To the degree
that a man is competent, he survives.
To the degree he is incompetent
he perishes.

Encourage
the attainment of competence
in any worthwhile pursuit.
Compliment it and reward it
whenever you find it.

Demand high performance standards.
The test of a society is whether or not you,
your family and friends can live in it safely.

The ingredients of competence include
observation, study and practice.

# 17-1.

## *L*ook.

See what you see, not what someone
tells you that you see.

What you observe is what *you* observe.
Look at things and life and others directly,
not through any cloud of prejudice,
curtain of fear or the interpretation of another.

Instead of arguing with others, get them to look.
The most flagrant lies can be punctured,
the greatest pretenses can be exposed,
the most intricate puzzles can resolve,
the most remarkable revelations can occur
simply by gently insisting that someone *look.*

When another finds things
almost too confusing and difficult to bear,
when his or her wits are going
around and around, get the person
to just stand back and look.

What they find is usually
very obvious when they see it.
Then they can go on and handle things.
But if they don't see it themselves,
observe it for themselves,
it may have little reality for them
and all the directives and orders
and punishment in the world
will not resolve their muddle.

One can indicate what direction
to look and suggest that they do look:
the conclusions are up to them.

A child or adult sees what he himself sees
and that is reality for him.

True competence is based on one's own
ability to observe. With that as reality,
only then can one be deft and sure.

# 17-2.
# _Learn._

Has there ever been an instance when
another had some false data about you?
Did it cause you trouble?

This can give you some idea of the havoc
false data can raise.

You could also have some
false data about another.

Separating the false from the true
brings about understanding.

There is a lot of false data around.
Evil-intentioned individuals manufacture it
to serve their own purposes. Some of it comes
from just plain ignorance of the facts.
It can block the acceptance
of true data.

The main process of learning consists of
inspecting the available data,
selecting the true from the false,
the important from the unimportant and
arriving thereby at conclusions
one makes and can apply.
If one does this, one is well on the way
to being competent.

The test of any "truth" is whether it is true
for *you.* If, when one has gotten the body of data,
cleared up any misunderstood words in it and
looked over the scene, it still doesn't seem true,
then it isn't true so far as you are concerned.
Reject it. And, if you like, carry it further
and conclude what the truth is for *you.*
After all, *you* are the one who is
going to have to use it or not use it,
think with it or not think with it.
If one blindly accepts "facts" or "truths"
just because he is told he must,
"facts" and "truths" which do not seem true to one,
or even false,
the end result can be an unhappy one.
That is the alley to the
trash bin of incompetence.

Another part of learning entails simply
committing things to memory—like the spelling
of words, mathematical tables and formulas,
the sequence of which buttons to push.
But even in simple memorizing
one has to know what the material is for
and how and when to use it.

The process of learning is not just
piling data on top of more data.
It is one of obtaining new understandings
and better ways to do things.

Those who get along in life
never really stop studying and learning.
The competent engineer keeps up with
new ways; the good athlete continually
reviews the progress of his sport;
any professional keeps a stack of his texts
to hand and consults them.

The new model
eggbeater or washing machine,
the latest year's car, all demand
some study and learning
before they can be
competently operated.
When people omit it,
there are accidents in the kitchen
and piles of bleeding wreckage
on the highways.

It is a very arrogant fellow who thinks
he has nothing further to learn in life.
It is a dangerously blind one
who cannot shed his prejudices
and false data and supplant them
with facts and truths
that can more fittingly assist
his own life and everyone else's.

There are ways to study so that one
really learns and can use what one learns.
In brief, it consists of having a teacher and/or
texts that know what they are talking about;
of clearing up every word one does not fully
understand; of consulting other references
and/or the scene of the subject; sorting out
the false data one might already have:
sifting the false from the true on the basis
of what is now true for you. The end result
will be certainty and potential competence.
It can be, actually, a bright and rewarding
experience. Not unlike climbing a treacherous
mountain through brambles but coming out
on top with a new view of the
whole wide world.

A civilization, to survive, must nurture
the habits and abilities to study in its schools.
A school is not a place where one puts children
to get them out from underfoot during the day.
That would be far too expensive for just that.
It is not a place where one manufactures parrots.
School is where one should learn to study and
where children can be prepared to come to grips
with reality, learn to handle it with competence
and be readied to take over tomorrow's world,
the world where current adults will be in their
later middle or old age.

The hardened criminal
never learned to learn. Repeatedly the courts
seek to teach him that if he commits
the crime again he will go back to prison:
most of them do the same crime again and go
back to prison. Factually, criminals cause
more and more laws to be passed:
the decent citizen is the one that obeys laws;
the criminals, by definition, do not:
criminals cannot learn.
Not all the orders and directives and punishments
and duress will work upon a being that
does not know how to learn and cannot learn.

A characteristic of a government that has
gone criminal—as has sometimes happened
in history—is that its leaders cannot learn:
all records and good sense may tell them that
disaster follows oppression; yet it has taken a
violent revolution to handle them or a
World War II to get rid of a Hitler and
those were very unhappy events for Mankind.
Such did not learn. They reveled in false data.
They refused all evidence and truth.
They had to be blown away.

The insane cannot learn.
Driven by hidden evil intentions or
crushed beyond the ability to reason,
facts and truth and reality are far beyond them.
They personify false data.
They will not or cannot really perceive or learn.

A multitude of personal and social problems
arise from the inability or refusal to learn.

The lives of some around you have
gone off the rails because they do not
know how to study, because they do not learn.
You can probably think of some examples.

If one cannot get those around him to
study and learn, one's own work can become
much harder and even overloaded and
one's own survival potential
can be greatly reduced.

One can help others
study and learn if only by
putting in their reach
the data they should have.
One can help simply by
acknowledging what they have learned.
One can assist if only by appreciating
any demonstrated increase in competence.
If one likes, one can do more than that:
another can be assisted by helping
them – without disputes – sort out false data,
by helping them find and clear up words
they have not understood,
by helping them find
and handle the reasons
they do not study and learn.

As life is largely trial and error,
instead of coming down on somebody
who makes a mistake, find out
how come a mistake was made and
see if the other can't learn something from it.

Now and then you may surprise
yourself by untangling a person's life just by
having gotten the person to study and learn.
I am sure you can think of many ways.
And I think you will find the gentler ones
work best. The world is brutal enough already
to people who can't learn.

# 17-3.
## *Practice.*[39]

Learning bears fruit when it is applied.
Wisdom, of course, can be pursued for its
own sake: there is even a kind of beauty in it.
But, truth told, one never really knows
if he is wise or not until he sees
the results of trying to apply it.

Any activity, skill or profession, ditch-digging,
law, engineering, cooking or whatever,
no matter how well studied, collides at last
with the acid test: can one DO it?
And that doing requires *practice.*

Movie stuntmen who don't practice first
get hurt. So do housewives.

39. *practice:* to exercise or perform repeatedly in order to acquire or polish a
skill.

Safety is not really a popular subject.
Because it is usually accompanied by
"be careful" and "go slow," people can feel
restraints are being put on them.
But there is another approach:
if one is really practiced, his skill and
dexterity is such that he doesn't have to
"be careful" or "go slow."
Safe high speed of motion
becomes possible only with practice.

One's skill and dexterity must be brought up
to match the speed of the age one lives in.
And that is done with practice.

One can train one's eyes, one's body,
one's hands and feet until, with practice,
they sort of "get to know."
One no longer has to "think" to set up the stove
or park the car: one just DOES it.
In any activity, quite a bit of what passes for
"talent" is really just *practice*.

Without working out
each movement one makes to do something
and then doing it over and over until one
can get it done without even thinking about it
and get it done with speed and accuracy,
one can set the stage for accidents.

Statistics tend to bear out that the
least practiced have the most accidents.

The same principle applies to crafts
and professions which mainly use the mind.
The lawyer who has not drill-drill-drilled
on courtroom procedure may not have learned
to shift his mental gears fast enough
to counter new turns of a case and loses it.
An undrilled new stockbroker
could lose a fortune in minutes.
A green salesman who has not rehearsed selling
can starve for lack of sales.
The right answer is to
practice, practice and practice!

Sometimes one finds that what one
has learned he cannot apply. If so, the faults lay
with improper study or with the teacher or text.
It is one thing to read the directions;
it is sometimes another thing entirely
to try to apply them.

Now and then, when one is
getting nowhere with practice, one has to
throw the book away and start from scratch.
The field of movie sound recording
has been like that: if one followed
what recordist texts there have been,
one couldn't get a bird song to sound any better
than a foghorn—that is why you can't tell
what the actors are saying in some movies.
The good sound recordist had to
work it all out for himself in order to do his job.
But in the same field of the cinema
there is a complete reverse of this:
several texts on cine lighting are excellent:
if followed exactly, one gets a beautiful scene.

It is regrettable, particularly
in a high-speed technical society,
that not all activities are adequately
covered with understandable texts.
But that should not stop one.
When good texts exist, value them
and study them well. Where they don't,
assemble what data is available,
study that and work the rest of it out.

But theory and data blossom only
when applied and applied with practice.

One is at risk when
those about one do not practice
their skills until they can really DO them.
There is a vast difference between "good enough"
and professional skill and dexterity.
The gap is bridged with *practice.*

Get people to look, study, work it out
and then do it. And when they have it right,
get them to practice, practice, practice
until they can do it like a pro.

There is considerable joy in skill,
dexterity and moving fast:
it can only be done safely with practice.
Trying to live in a high-speed world
with low-speed people is not very safe.

*The way to happiness*
*is best traveled with competent companions.*

# 18.

## RESPECT THE RELIGIOUS BELIEFS OF OTHERS.

*T*olerance is a
good cornerstone on which to build
human relationships. When one views
the slaughter and suffering caused by
religious intolerance down all the history of Man
and into modern times, one can see
that intolerance is a very non-survival activity.

Religious tolerance does not mean
one cannot express his own beliefs.
It does mean that seeking to undermine
or attack the religious faith and beliefs of another
has always been a short road to trouble.

Philosophers since the times of
ancient Greece have disputed with one another
about the nature of God, Man and the universe.
The opinions of authorities ebb and flow:
just now the philosophies of "mechanism"[40] and
"materialism"[41] — dating as far back as
Ancient Egypt and Greece — are the fad:
they seek to assert that all is matter and
overlook that, neat as their explanations
of evolution may be, they still do not rule out
*additional* factors that might be at work,
that might be merely using such things as evolution.
They are today the "official" philosophies
and are even taught in schools.
They have their own zealots who attack
the beliefs and religions of others:
the result can be intolerance and contention.

40. *mechanism:* the view that all life is only matter in motion and can be totally explained by physical laws. Advanced by Leucippus and Democritus (460 B.C. to 370 B.C.) who may have gotten it from Egyptian mythology. Upholders of this philosophy felt they had to neglect religion because they could not reduce it to mathematics. They were attacked by religious interests and in their turn attacked religions. Robert Boyle (1627–1691), who developed Boyle's Law in physics, refuted it by raising the question as to whether or not nature might have designs such as matter in motion.

41. *materialism:* any one of a family of metaphysical theories which view the universe as consisting of hard objects such as stones, big or very small. The theories seek to explain away such things as minds by saying they can be reduced to physical things or their motions. Materialism is a very ancient idea. There are other ideas.

If all the brightest minds since the
fifth century B.C. or before have never been able to
agree on the subject of religion or anti-religion,
it is an arena of combat between people
that one would do well to stay out of.

In this sea of contention,
one bright principle has emerged:
the right to believe as one chooses.

"Faith" and "belief"
do not necessarily surrender to logic:
they cannot even be declared to be illogical.
They can be things quite apart.

Any advice one might
give another on this subject
is safest when it simply asserts the right
to believe as one chooses. One is at liberty
to hold up his own beliefs for acceptance.
One is at risk when he seeks to assault
the beliefs of others, much more so when
he attacks and seeks to harm them because
of their religious convictions.

Man, since the dawn of the species,
has taken great consolation and joy
in his religions. Even the "mechanist" and
"materialist" of today sound much like
the priests of old as they spread their dogma.

Men without faith are a pretty sorry lot.
They can even be given something to have faith in.
But when they have religious beliefs,
respect them.

*The way to happiness can become*
*contentious when one fails to respect*
*the religious beliefs*
*of others.*

# 19.

## TRY NOT TO DO THINGS TO OTHERS THAT YOU WOULD NOT LIKE THEM TO DO TO YOU.

*A*mong
many peoples in many lands
for many ages there have been versions
of what is called "The Golden Rule."[42]
The above is a wording of it
that relates to harmful acts.

42. *"The Golden Rule":* although this is looked upon by Christians as
Christian and is found in the New and Old Testaments, many other races
and peoples spoke of it. It also appears in the *Analects* of Confucius
(fifth and sixth centuries B.C.) who himself quoted from more ancient works.
It is also found in "primitive" tribes. In one form or another it appears in
the ancient works of Plato, Aristotle, Isocrates and Seneca. For thousands of
years it has been held by Man as a standard of ethical conduct. The versions
given in this book are newly worded however, as in earlier wordings it was
thought to be too idealistic to be kept. It is possible to keep this version.

Only a saint
could go through life
without ever harming another.
But only a criminal
hurts those around him
without a second thought.

Completely aside
from feelings of "guilt"
or "shame" or "conscience,"
all of which can be real enough
and bad enough, it also happens to be true
that the harm one does to others
can recoil on oneself.

Not all harmful acts are reversible:
one can commit an act against another
which cannot be waived aside or forgotten.
Murder is such an act.
One can work out how severe violation
of almost any precept in this book
could become an irreversible harmful act
against another.

The ruin of another's life can wreck one's own.
Society reacts—the prisons and the insane asylums
are stuffed with people who harmed their fellows.
But there are other penalties:
whether one is caught or not,
committing harmful acts against others,
particularly when hidden, can cause one to
suffer severe changes in his attitudes
toward others and himself,
all of them unhappy ones.
The happiness and joy of life depart.

This version of
"The Golden Rule" is also useful as a test.
When one persuades someone to apply it, the
person can attain a reality on what a harmful act *is*.
It answers for one what *harm* is.
The philosophic question concerning *wrongdoing,*
the argument of what is wrong
is answered at once on a personal basis:
Would you not like that to happen to you? No?
Then it must be a harmful action and,
from society's viewpoint, a wrong action.
It can awaken social consciousness.
It can then let one work out what one should do
and what one should not do.

In a time when some feel
no restraint from doing harmful acts,
the survival potential of the individual
sinks to a very low ebb.

If you can persuade people to
apply this, you will have given them a precept
by which they can evaluate their own lives
and, for some, opened the door to
let them rejoin the human race.

*The way to happiness is closed*
*to those who do not restrain themselves*
*from committing harmful acts.*

# 20.

## TRY TO TREAT OTHERS AS YOU WOULD WANT THEM TO TREAT YOU.

*T*his is a positive
version of "The Golden Rule."

Don't be surprised if someone seems
to resent being told to "be good."
But the resentment may not
come at all at the idea of "being good":
it may be because the person factually
has a misunderstanding of
what it means.

One can get into a lot of
conflicting opinions and confusions
about what "good behavior" might be.
One might never have grasped—even if
the teacher did—why he or she was given
the grade received for "conduct."
One might even have been given
or assumed false data concerning it:
"children should be seen and not heard,"
"being good means being inactive."

However, there is a way to clear it all up
to one's complete satisfaction.

In all times and in most places,
Mankind has looked up to
and revered certain values.
They are called the virtues.[43]
They have been attributed to wise men,
holy men, saints and gods.
They have made the difference between
a barbarian and a cultured person,
the difference between chaos
and a decent society.

43. *virtues:* the ideal qualities in good human conduct.

It doesn't absolutely require
a heavenly mandate nor a tedious search
through the thick tomes of the philosophers
to discover what "good" is.
A self-revelation can occur
on the subject.

It can be worked out
by almost any person.

If one were to think over how he or she
would like to be treated by others,
one would evolve the human virtues.
Just figure out how you would want
people to treat *you*.

You would possibly,
first of all, want to be treated *justly:*
you wouldn't want people lying about you
or falsely or harshly condemning you.
Right?

You would probably want your friends
and companions to be *loyal:*
you would not want them to betray you.

You could want to be treated
with *good sportsmanship,* not hoodwinked
nor tricked.

You would want people to
be *fair* in their dealings with you.
You would want them to be *honest*
with you and not cheat you.
Correct?

You might want
to be treated *kindly* and
without cruelty.

You would possibly
want people to be *considerate* of
your rights and feelings.

When you were down,
you might like others to
be *compassionate.*

Instead of blasting you,
you would probably want others
to exhibit *self-control.*
Right?

If you had any defects
or shortcomings, if you made a mistake,
you might want people to be *tolerant,*
not critical.

Rather than concentrating
on censure and punishment, you would
prefer people were *forgiving.*
Correct?

You might want people
to be *benevolent* toward you,
not mean nor stingy.

Your possible desire would be
for others to *believe in you,* not doubt you
at every hand.

You would probably
prefer to be given *respect,*
not insulted.

Possibly you would
want others to be *polite* to you
and also treat you with *dignity.*
Right?

You might like
people to *admire* you.

When you did something
for them you would possibly
like people to *appreciate* you.
Correct?

You would probably
like others to be *friendly*
toward you.

From some you might
want *love*.

And above all,
you wouldn't want these people
just pretending these things,
you would want them to be quite real
in their attitudes and to be
acting with *integrity.*

You could possibly
think of others.
And there are the precepts
contained in this book.
But above you would have
worked out the summary of
what are called
the *virtues.*

It requires no
great stretch of imagination
for one to recognize that if
he were to be treated that way regularly
by others around him, his life would
exist on a pleasant level.
And it is doubtful if one would build up
much animosity toward those
who treated him in this fashion.

Now there is
an interesting phenomenon[44]
at work in human relations.
When one person yells at another,
the other has an impulse to yell back.
One is treated pretty much
the way he treats others:
one actually sets an example
of how he should be treated.
A is mean to B so B is mean to A.
A is friendly to B so B is friendly to A.
I am sure you have seen this at work continually.
George hates all women so women
tend to hate George.
Carlos acts tough to everyone so others
tend to act tough toward Carlos—and if they
don't dare out in the open,
they privately may nurse a hidden impulse
to act very tough indeed toward Carlos
if they ever get a chance.

44. *phenomenon:* an observable fact or event.

In the unreal world of fiction
and the motion pictures, one sees polite villains
with unbelievably efficient gangs and lone heroes
who are outright boors.[45] Life really isn't like that:
real villains are usually pretty crude people
and their henchmen cruder; Napoleon and Hitler
were betrayed right and left by their own people.
Real heroes are the quietest-talking fellows
you ever met and they are very polite
to their friends.

When one is lucky enough to get to meet
and talk to the men and women who are
at the top of their professions, one is struck
by an observation often made that they are
just about the nicest people you ever met.
That is one of the reasons they are at the top:
they try, most of them, to treat others well.
And those around them respond and
tend to treat them well and even forgive
their few shortcomings.

45. *boor:* a person with rude, clumsy manners and little refinement.

All right: one can work out for himself
the human virtues just by recognizing how he
himself would like to be treated. And from that,
I think you will agree, one has settled any
confusions as to what "good conduct" really is.
It's a far cry from being inactive, sitting still with
your hands in your lap and saying nothing.
"Being good" can be a very active
and powerful force.

There is little joy to be found in gloomy,
restrained solemnity. When some of old
made it seem that to practice virtue required
a grim and dismal sort of life, they tended to
infer that all pleasure came from being wicked:
nothing could be further from the facts.
Joy and pleasure do *not* come from immorality!
Quite the reverse! Joy and pleasure arise only in
honest hearts: the immoral lead unbelievably
tragic lives filled with suffering and pain.
The human virtues have little to do
with gloominess. They are the
bright face of life itself.

Now what do you suppose
would happen if one were to
try to treat those around him with
*justness,*
*loyalty,*
*good sportsmanship,*
*fairness,*
*honesty,*
*kindness,*
*consideration,*
*compassion,*
*self-control,*
*tolerance,*
*forgivingness,*
*benevolence,*
*belief,*
*respect,*
*politeness,*
*dignity,*
*admiration,*
*friendliness,*
*love,*
and did it with *integrity?*

It might take a while but don't you
suppose that many others would then begin
to try to treat one the same way?

Even allowing for
the occasional lapses—the news
that startles one half out of his wits,
the burglar one has to bop on the head,
the nut who is driving slow in the fast lane
when one is late for work—it should be
fairly visible that one would lift oneself
to a new plane of human relations.
One's survival potential
would be considerably raised.
And certainly one's life
would be a happier one.

One *can* influence the
conduct of others around him.
If one is not like that already,
it can be made much easier by just
picking one virtue a day and
specializing in it for that day.
Doing that, they would all
eventually be in.

Aside from personal benefit,
one can take a hand, no matter how small,
in beginning a new era for human relations.

The pebble, dropped in a pool,
can make ripples to the furthest shore.

*The way to happiness
is made much brighter
by applying the precept,
"Try to treat others as you
would want them to treat you."*

# 21.

# FLOURISH[46]
# AND PROSPER.[47]

*S*ometimes others
seek to crush one down, to make nothing
out of one's hopes and dreams,
one's future and oneself.

By ridicule and many other means,
another who is evil-intentioned
toward one can try to bring about
one's decline.

46. *flourish:* to be in a state of activity and production; expanding in
influence; thriving; visibly doing well.
47. *prosper:* to achieve economic success; succeeding at what one does.

For whatever reason,
efforts to improve oneself,
to become happier in life,
can become the subject of attacks.

It is sometimes necessary
to handle such directly.
But there is a long-range handling
that seldom fails.

What, exactly,
are such people trying to do to one?
They are trying to reduce one downward.

They must conceive that one is
dangerous to them in some way:
that if one got up in the world,
one could be a menace to them.
So, in various ways, such seek to
depress one's talents
and capabilities.

Some madmen
even have a general plan
that goes like this:
"If A becomes more successful,
A could be a menace to me;
therefore I must do all I can
to make A less successful."
It never seems to occur to such
that their actions might make
an enemy out of A even though
he was no enemy before.
It can be classed as an almost certain way
for such madmen to get into trouble.
Some do it just from prejudice
or because they "don't like someone."

But however it is attempted,
the real object of such
is to make their target
grow less and fail in life.

The real handling
of such a situation and such people,
the real way to defeat them
is to flourish and prosper.

Oh, yes, it is true that such people,
seeing one improve his lot,
can become frantic
and attack all the harder.
The thing to do is
handle them if one must
but don't give up
flourishing and prospering,
for that is what such people
want you to do.

If you
flourish and prosper
more and more,
such people
go into apathy about it:
they can give it up completely.

If one's aims in life
are worthwhile,
if one carries them out
with some attention
to the precepts in this book,
if one flourishes and prospers,
one certainly will
wind up the victor.
And, hopefully,
without harming
a single hair on their heads.

*And that is my wish for you:*
*flourish and prosper!*

# EPILOGUE

*H*appiness lies
in engaging in worthwhile activities.
But there is only one person who for certain
can tell what will make one happy—oneself.

The precepts given in this book
are really the edges of the road:
violating them, one is like the motorist who
plunges off onto the verge—the result can be
wreckage of the moment, the relationship, a life.

Only you can say where the road goes
for one sets his goals for the hour,
for the relationship, for the phase of life.

One can feel at times like a spinning leaf blown
along a dirty street, one can feel like a grain of
sand stuck in one place. But nobody has said
that life was a calm and orderly thing: it isn't.
One isn't a tattered leaf nor a grain of sand:
one can, to greater or lesser degree
draw his road map and follow it.

One can feel that things are such now
that it is much too late to do anything,
that one's past road is so messed up that
there is no chance of drawing a future one
that will be any different:
there is always a point on the road
when one can map a new one.
And try to follow it.
There is no person alive
who cannot make a new beginning.

It can be said without the slightest fear
of contradiction that others may mock one
and seek by various means to push one
onto the verge, to tempt one in various ways
to lead an immoral life: all such persons do so
to accomplish private ends of their own
and one will wind up, if one heeds them,
in tragedy and sorrow.

Of course one will have occasional loses
trying to apply this book and get it applied.
One should just learn from these and carry on.
Who said the road doesn't have bumps?

It can still be traveled.
So people can fall down:
it doesn't mean they can't
get up again and keep going.

If one keeps the edges on the road,
one can't go far wrong.
True excitement, happiness and joy
come from other things,
not from broken lives.

If you can get others to follow the road,
you yourself will be free enough
to give yourself a chance
to discover what real happiness is.

*The way to happiness is a high-speed road
to those who know where the edges are.*

You're the driver.

Fare well.

# EDITOR'S GLOSSARY
## OF WORDS, TERMS & PHRASES

*Words often have several meanings. The definitions used here only give the meaning that the word has as it is used in this book. Beside each definition you will find the page on which it first appears, so you can refer back to the text if you wish. Definitions appearing as footnotes, throughout the book, were written by the author and are included below for ease of reference.*

*— The Editors*

**abroad:** in circulation throughout a country or area; widely current. Page 64.

**academic:** of or relating to a school or other educational institutions. Page 48.

**acid test:** a final or deciding test to establish value, effectiveness, genuineness, etc. (*Acid* is a strong substance capable of dissolving things such as various metals.) The term dates back to the 1800s, when acid was used to distinguish gold from cheap metal which appeared to be gold. The acid would corrode such metals as iron or copper, but would do nothing to real gold. Page 140.

**adamant:** hard; not giving in; unyielding; something which won't break; insistent; refusing any other opinion; surrendering to nothing. (From *author's footnote.*) Page 59.

**a little (something) goes a long way:** a small amount of something can have a great effect or strong influence with somebody or something. Page 20.

**alley:** a path or course of action. An *alley* is a narrow passageway or lane, especially one running between or behind buildings. Page 126.

**all manner of:** many different kinds of; all sorts of. Page 100.

**all the:** to that extent; that much, as in *"Oh, yes, it is true that such people, seeing one improve his lot, can become frantic and attack all the harder."* Page 198.

**analects:** selections from the writings of an author and often used as a title, especially when published as a collection, as in *"the Analects of Confucius."* Page 159.

**animosity:** a feeling of strong dislike or active hatred. Page 183.

**appeal:** an earnest or urgent request to somebody for something, such as aid or support. Page 40.

**aristocracy:** government by a few with special privileges, ranks or positions; rule by an elite few who are above the general law; a group who by birth or position are "superior to everybody else" and who can make or apply laws to others but consider they themselves are not affected by the laws. (From *author's footnote.*) Page 60.

**Aristotle:** (384–322 B.C.) Greek philosopher, educator and scientist, considered the most scholarly and learned of the ancient Greek philosophers. His works covered all branches of human knowledge known in his time, including logic, ethics, natural science and politics. Page 159.

**as far (back) as:** to the same degree or extent that, as in *"dating as far back as Ancient Egypt and Greece."* Page 152.

**asylums:** institutions for the care of people who are deemed "mentally ill" e.g., because of harm they brought to self or others. Page 161.

**at every hand:** constantly, on every occasion or in every case. *Hand* is used here to mean direction or side and is a reference to the position of the hands—one on either side of the body. Page 176.

**at the mercy of:** without any protection against; entirely in the power of, or helpless before. Page 54.

# B

**babyhood:** the period of time when someone is a baby, especially before he or she can walk. (*Hood* is added to a word to show a period of time or a state or condition.) Page 36.

**back:** in or into the past; ago, as in *"dating as far back as Ancient Egypt and Greece."* Page 152.

**barbarian:** an uncivilized person, one without culture, refinement or education. Page 167.

**barbaric:** of, relating to or characteristic of a *barbarian,* one without culture, refinement or education. Also characteristic of people belonging to a wild or cruel group or society. Page 76.

**bear false witness:** to tell lies or state something false while under oath or in a court of law; to state falsely. *Bear* means to give or provide. *Witness* means swearing to a fact, statement, etc.; proof or evidence. Page 50.

**bearing:** the manner in which one behaves or conducts oneself. Page 69.

**bear out:** support, back up or confirm; prove. Page 144.

**bears fruit:** produces the intended or desired result or effect. *Bears* means brings forth or produces, as by natural growth, and *fruit* means that which is produced, a result, effect or outcome. Page 140.

**benevolent:** showing kindness or goodwill, desiring to help others; generous. Page 176.

**benign:** tending to be beneficial in nature or influence or productive of a favorable result. Page 67.

**blank slate:** something new, fresh, unmarked or uninfluenced. A *slate* is a sheet of dark colored rock, split into a thin flat plate and used to write on with a sharp pointed instrument or chalk. A *blank slate* is thus one which is without any writing or marking on it and is ready to be written on. Page 32.

**blasting:** criticizing (something or somebody) very strongly; attacking forcefully. Page 172.

**boor:** a person with rude, clumsy manners and little refinement. (From *author's footnote.*) Page 186.

**Boyle's Law:** a law stating that the pressure of a gas, at a constant temperature, increases as the volume decreases. For example, when a gas (such as normal air) is put into a container, its volume (how much space it is occupying) and the pressure it exerts against the inside of the container are related to each other. If the volume is reduced by squashing the air into a smaller space, the pressure increases. If the volume is increased, such as by putting the same amount of air into a larger container, the pressure is less. Boyle's Law was named after Irish physicist Robert Boyle (1627–1691) who formulated it in 1662. Page 152.

**brambles:** any rough, thorny vines or shrubs. Page 130.

**brink:** literally, the extreme edge of something. Hence, the point at which something begins, as in *"from babyhood to the brink of adult life."* Page 36.

**broken:** destroyed, damaged or badly hurt, as if by breaking. Page 206.

**Buddhism:** a world religion based on the teachings of Siddhartha Gautama Buddha (563–483? B.C.) and holding that a state of enlightenment can be attained by overcoming worldly desires. Buddha means "Enlightened One." Page 26.

**building block:** literally, a large block of concrete or similar hard material used for building houses and other large structures. Hence, anything thought of as a basic unit of construction, such as an element or component regarded as contributing to the growth or development of something. Page 98.

**bungling:** the activity of careless or clumsy actions or making mistakes. Page 117.

**buy:** to gain the support or obedience of, as in *"to 'buy' the child with an overwhelm of toys and possessions."* Page 32.

**cannot help but:** to be impossible or unable to prevent or avoid something, as in *"If the child is frank and honest, there cannot help but be an appeal that will reach."* Page 40.

**case(s): 1.** the actual state of things, as in *"This is not now the case, if it ever was."* Page 24.
**2.** an instance of something; an occurrence; an example, as in *"some are even born as drug addicts: but such cases are an unusual few."* Page 32.
**3.** a matter examined or judged in a court of law, as in *"The lawyer who has not drill-drill-drilled on courtroom procedure may not have learned to shift his mental gears fast enough to counter new turns of a case and loses it."* Page 144.

**censure:** an expression of strong disapproval or harsh criticism. Page 174.

**chaotic:** having the character or nature of total disorder or confusion. (From *author's footnote.*) Page 7.

**cine:** abbreviation for *cinematography,* the skill or art of movie (motion picture) photography. Page 146.

**civics:** the study of the principles and structure of government (in its relationship to citizens). Page 66.

**codify:** arrange and classify, especially laws, into an organized, comprehensible system. Page 60.

**coins:** figuratively, things given or offered in exchange for something else; something accepted as having value. From the literal definition, being pieces of metal (gold, silver, copper, etc.) of definite value, used as money. Page 104.

**come to grips with:** to begin to understand and deal with directly or firmly. *Grip* means the grasping of something tightly and in this sense refers to a mental or intellectual hold on something. Page 132.

**coming down on:** criticizing or punishing someone severely. Page 138.

**commercial:** having to do with or engaged in *commerce,* the buying and selling of goods or services, as opposed to religious, educational, charitable, etc. Page 26.

**committing something to memory:** learning things well enough to remember them exactly. *Committing* in this sense means transferring something to (a state or place). Page 128.

**commotion:** agitated and noisy activity, confusion or disturbance. Page 59.

**communicable:** (said of a disease) able to be passed from one person to another; contagious. Page 13.

**competent:** able to do well those things one does; capable; skilled in doing what one does; measuring up to the demands of one's activities. (From *author's footnote.*) Page 117.

**compromise:** a settlement of differences in which each side gives in on some point while retaining others and reaching a mutual agreement thereby. (From *author's footnote.*) Page 40.

**considerable:** large in amount, extent or degree. Page 50.

**consolation:** that which comforts or cheers the mind or spirit or alleviates distress or misery. Page 155.

**contention:** a state of angry disagreement and disharmony between people. Page 152.

**contentious:** causing or likely to cause argument, conflict or severe difference of opinion. Page 156.

**cornerstone:** literally, a stone that forms the base of a corner of a building joining two walls. Hence, a fundamentally important basis on which things are constructed or developed. Page 151.

**crafts:** activities, professions or occupations that require the application of artistic skill and training, experience or specialized knowledge. Page 144.

**credit:** something that is worthy of praise, recognition or acknowledgment. Page 103.

**crude:** lacking culture, refinement, etc.; offensive or rude. Page 186.

**cultured:** improved by education; having refined taste, speech and manners. Page 167.

**curtain of fear:** a *curtain* is something that hides or masks, or which blocks clear perception, understanding or communication. Hence, a *curtain of fear* is a barrier that makes one afraid to view or understand something or someone directly or accurately. Page 120.

# D

**dawn of the species:** the first appearance or beginning of Mankind on Earth. *Dawn* means the beginning (of something) or the initial stage of a developmental process and *species* is the human race. Page 155.

**deference:** courteous, respectful regard for another; polite respect, especially putting another's interests first. Page 39.

**deft:** demonstrating skill and cleverness. Also, skillful and quick in one's movements. Page 122.

**degraded:** reduced far below ordinary standards of civilized life and conduct. Page 76.

**delusion:** a fixed false belief; a perception that is perceived in a way different from the way it is in reality. From the word *delude,* which means to mislead the mind or judgment of, and *illusion,* which means something that deceives by producing a false or misleading impression of reality. Page 19.

**Democritus:** (460–370 B.C.) Greek philosopher, who developed the atomic theory of the universe, which had been originated by his teacher, the philosopher Leucippus. According to Democritus, all things are composed of minute, invisible, indestructible particles of pure matter which move about eternally in infinite empty space. Democritus believed that our world came about from the chance combination of atoms. Page 152.

**destiny:** the apparently predetermined course of events considered as something beyond human power or control. Page 118.

**deter:** to prevent or discourage. (From *author's footnote.*) Page 20.

**dexterity:** skill and ease in physical movement, especially in the use of the hands. Also, mental skill; cleverness. Page 142.

**dictator:** a ruler whose word is law, and who has total, unrestricted control in a government and typically rules with harsh or cruel actions and ruthless suppression of opposition. Page 64.

**dilemma:** a situation in which one has to make a difficult choice between two, or sometimes more than two actions, none of which seem to be satisfactory solutions. Page 106.

**discharge:** to release or free from (a debt, obligation, duty, etc.) by paying or performing some task. Page 104.

**disfigured:** having the appearance of being damaged; spoiled or ruined. Page 77.

**disposition:** the combination of qualities that form one's normal frame of mind or characteristic attitude. Page 69.

**disservice:** an action that causes harm or difficulty; the opposite of service, which is work done for somebody else to help them or as a favor. Page 104.

**dogma:** a set of beliefs, opinions, principles, etc., that are laid down and held as true and not subject to question. From the Greek word *dogma,* opinion. Page 155.

**dole:** the British term for government relief. (From *author's footnote.*) Page 111.

**duress:** compulsion to do or not to do something resulting from pressure, force or threats. Page 134.

# E

**ebb and flow:** literally, the moving of the tide out to sea (ebb) and its alternate movement towards land (flow). *Tide* is the periodic variation in the surface level of the oceans, most noticeable at the shoreline. Hence, a recurrent or rhythmical pattern of coming and going, or decline and renewed advance, ups and downs, etc. Page 152.

**economic:** of or relating to *economics,* the social science that studies the production, distribution and consumption (using) of commodities (things). The word originally meant the science or art of managing a house or household. Page 88.

**ends:** the goals, objects or purposes an individual or group intends to achieve. Page 44.

**ends, suit their own:** satisfy or please their own intentions or desires (to the exclusion of others). *Suit* means satisfy, please or agree with the views or wishes of, and *ends* means the things an individual or group has for goals or intends to achieve. Page 48.

**engaging (in):** involving oneself or becoming occupied (in); participating (in). Page 203.

**enhance:** intensify, increase or further improve the quality or extent of. Page 3.

**environment:** one's surroundings; the material things around one; the area one lives in; the living things, objects, spaces and forces with which one lives whether close to or far away. (From *author's footnote.*) Page 29.

**epilogue:** a short addition or concluding section at the end of a literary work. Page 203.

**era:** a portion or length of time marked by particular circumstances, distinctive characteristics, events, persons, etc. Page 86.

**esteemed:** held in high regard; admired, respected or valued. Page 98.

**evolutionary:** related to a very ancient theory that all plants and animals developed from simpler forms and were shaped by their surroundings rather than being planned or created. (From *author's footnote*.) Page 30.

**example:** someone or something worthy of imitation or duplication; a pattern, a model. (From *author's footnote*.) Page 43.

**eyesore:** something that is unpleasant or offensively ugly to look at. Page 76.

**face of, in the:** when confronted with. Page 26.

**far cry:** quite some distance; a long way; hence only remotely related; very different. Page 187.

**fare well:** used to express good wishes on parting. *Fare* means to get along or experience good fortune. Page 206.

**fashion, in this:** in the way or manner indicated. Page 183.

**firm:** a company or business. Page 59.

**flagrant:** shockingly noticeable or evident; obvious. Page 120.

**floods:** very large numbers of things, likened to a *flood,* a large quantity of water overflowing onto land. Page 24.

**flourish:** to be in a state of activity and production; expanding in influence; thriving; visibly doing well. (From *author's footnote*.) Page 195.

**foghorn:** a very loud, deep-sounding horn set off on a ship or boat when fog reduces visibility, as a warning to other vessels. Page 146.

**formula(s):** in mathematics, a rule or principle represented in symbols, numbers or letters, often equating one thing to another. Example: To calculate the area of a rectangle (a carpet for instance) one uses the formula of A x B = C, where A stands for the length, B the width and C the area. Page 128.

**foul:** make something dirty or impure; pollute. Page 82.

**from scratch:** from a position of no previous advantage or knowledge; from nothing. A *scratch* is a line or mark drawn as an indication of a starting point in some sporting contest. Page 146.

**fruit, bears:** produces the intended or desired result or effect. *Bears* means brings forth or produces, as by natural growth, and *fruit* means that which is produced, a result, effect or outcome. Page 140.

# G

**geared:** equipped or adapted so as to make suitable for a particular purpose or situation. Page 59.

**gears, shift (his) mental:** change one's ideas, conceptual approach, etc., in handling something such as a problem or situation. The phrase refers to the gears of an automobile which the driver shifts depending upon the speed required due to conditions such as hills, traffic, etc. Page 144.

**gift of heaven:** a gift granted to Mankind from a divine power or source. Hence, something very special, significant or important. Page 118.

**gloom:** act, look or feel miserable, sad and hopeless. Page 111.

**goes a long way, a little (something):** a small amount of something can have a great effect or strong influence with somebody or something. Page 20.

**"Golden Rule, The":** although this is looked upon by Christians as Christian and is found in the New and Old Testaments, many other races and peoples spoke of it. It also appears in the *Analects* of Confucius (fifth and sixth centuries B.C.) who himself quoted from more ancient works. It is also found in "primitive" tribes. In one form or another it appears in the ancient works of Plato, Aristotle, Isocrates and Seneca. For thousands of years it has been held by Man as a standard of ethical conduct. The versions given in this book are newly worded however, as in earlier wordings it was thought to be too idealistic to be kept. It is possible to keep this version. (From *author's footnote.*) Page 159.

**go to pieces:** become upset or nervous to the extent that one cannot live, work or perform as one should; to be ruined or wrecked, likened to something breaking up into fragments. Page 86.

**got up in the world:** became more important, successful or prosperous in society. Page 196.

**grade:** a mark or rating on examinations and in school courses, indicating the relative quality of a student's work in school. In US schools, for example, the grade system consists of a scale starting at the bottom with F (failing) and moving up through D (poor or barely passing), C (average or satisfactory), B (good or above average), and A (excellent). Page 166.

**green:** young, new, recent or fresh; untrained or inexperienced. Page 144.

**grips with, come to:** to begin to understand and deal with directly or firmly. *Grip* means the grasping of something tightly and in this sense refers to a mental or intellectual hold on something. Page 132.

**ground glass (in the soup):** a reference to the practice of committing murder by grinding up glass so fine that it is unnoticeable when placed in food and damages the digestive system of the victim beyond repair when ingested. Page 24.

# H

**hand, at every:** constantly, on every occasion or in every case. *Hand* is used here to mean direction or side and is a reference to the position of the hands—one on either side of the body. Page 176.

**happiness:** a condition or state of well-being, contentment, pleasure; joyful, cheerful, untroubled existence; the reaction to having nice things happen to one. (From *author's footnote.*) Page 7.

**hardened:** firmly established or unlikely to change. Page 134.

**have had it:** to be in a state considered beyond remedy, repair or salvage; to have had an (unfavorable) outcome finally decided. Page 82.

**havoc:** great confusion, disorder or chaos; destruction. Page 124.

**heavenly mandate:** a *mandate* is an authoritative command, instruction or order. A *heavenly mandate* would be a direction or command coming from a god. Page 168.

**heeds:** pays attention to; listens to and considers. Page 204.

**henchmen:** loyal supporters or followers of criminals or corrupt political leaders. Page 186.

**hide-outs:** places where someone can stay out of view or disappear, especially someone wanted by the police, etc. Page 92.

**high road:** a direct or certain route or course; the surest path. Page 114.

**Hitler:** Adolf Hitler (1889–1945), German political leader of the twentieth century who dreamed of creating a master race that would rule for a thousand years as the third German empire. Taking over rule of Germany by force in 1933 as a dictator, he began World War II (1939–1945), subjecting much of Europe to his domination and murdering millions of Jews and others considered "inferior." During his rule, several unsuccessful attempts by German officers were made to assassinate him. Hitler committed suicide in 1945 when Germany's defeat was close at hand. Page 134.

**hold to:** to remain attached or faithful to; refuse to abandon or change (a principle or opinion). Page 30.

**holy:** dedicated to God or a religious purpose; living according to a strict or highly moral, religious or spiritual system, as in *"holy men."* Page 167.

**honor:** to show respect for; to treat with deference and courtesy. (From *author's footnote.*) Page 39.

**hoodwinked:** deceived by false appearance or fooled; prevented from seeing the truth or facts, as if blindfolded mentally. A *hood* is a loose covering placed over the head which sometimes blocks vision. *Hoodwink* originally meant to blindfold. Page 170.

**humanities:** branches of learning concerned with human thought and relations, especially literature, philosophy, history, etc., and as distinguished from the physical sciences. Page 117.

# I

**ill-:** used in combination with another word with the meaning of badly, wrongly or imperfectly, as in *"ill-tempered"* or *"ill-planned."* Page 14.

**ill-tempered:** having or showing a bad or irritable mood or outlook. Page 14.

**illustrations:** examples serving to explain, clarify or prove something. Page 53.

**immoral:** not moral; not following good practices of behavior; not doing right; lacking any idea of proper conduct. (From *author's footnote.*) Page 7.

**imperils:** puts at risk of being harmed, injured or destroyed. Page 63.

**implacable:** not open to being quieted, soothed or pleased; remorseless; relentless. (From *author's footnote.*) Page 59.

**incompetence:** lacking adequate knowledge or skill or ability; unskilled; incapable; subject to making big errors or mistakes; bungling. (From *author's footnote.*) Page 117.

**incompetence, trash bin of:** figuratively, a place where inability, lack of skill or ineffectiveness are dumped and stored. From *trash bin* meaning a container where refuse, garbage, unwanted or worthless material or objects are disposed of. Page 126.

**incurs:** acquires or comes into something, usually undesirable; becomes burdened with something such as a debt. Page 103.

**industrious:** applying oneself with energy to study or work; actively and purposefully getting things done; opposite of being idle and accomplishing nothing. (From *author's footnote.*) Page 111.

**influence:** the resulting effect. (From *author's footnote.*) Page 43.

**influences:** has an effect upon. (From *author's footnote*.) Page 43.

**inherent:** existing in someone's internal character as a permanent and inseparable element, quality or attribute. Page 33.

**in its own time and place:** during that specified time period and location. The use of *own* emphasizes the idea of a specific environment and time (in this case, the late 1700s and early 1800s in the United States, France and South America). Page 60.

**in spite of:** regardless of; without being affected by the particular factor mentioned. Page 41.

**interpersonal:** of or having to do with the relations between persons. Page 50.

**in the face of:** when confronted with. Page 26.

**in the long run:** concerning a longer period in the future; in the end. Page 34.

**in the open:** not hidden or secret; so as to be seen. Page 184.

**in this fashion:** in the way or manner indicated. Page 183.

**intricate:** containing many small parts that are skillfully made or assembled; very complicated. Page 117.

**Isocrates:** (436–338 B.C.) Greek author, educator and follower of Plato, known for his many great orations (formal public speeches or lectures) which he published in pamphlet form. He founded a school where he taught young men from all parts of the Greek-speaking world the arts of writing essays and of public speaking (oratory). His pupils included orators, historians, debaters and writers. Page 159.

**keeps up with:** remains informed and up-to-date about something that undergoes continuous change or progress, as in *"The competent engineer keeps up with new ways."* Page 128.

**law codes:** systematically arranged and very thorough collections of laws, rules or regulations. Page 57.

**lay:** belong to or are attached to (some thing, person, etc.); exist or can be found in (some thing, person, etc.). Page 146.

**laying down:** establishing or formulating definitely a rule, principle, etc.; firmly recommending a course of action, limits, etc. Page 34.

**lay (oneself) open to:** expose oneself to or leave oneself without adequate protection from danger or harm. Page 24.

**legendary:** very well known, especially over time, likened to a legend, an old, well-known story. Page 111.

**legislative bodies:** groups of people, usually elected, who have the responsibility and authority to make, change or abolish laws for a country or state. Page 57.

**Leucippus:** Greek philosopher (ca. 450–370 B.C.) who believed that all matter was made up of atoms, that all observable properties of an object result from the behavior of these atoms, and that this behavior of atoms was completely determined in advance. His teachings were further developed by his pupil, the Greek philosopher Democritus. Page 152.

**liberty, at:** free to do or be as specified; allowed without restriction. Page 155.

**lies:** false statements or pieces of information deliberately presented as being true; a falsehood; anything meant to deceive or give a wrong impression. (From *author's footnote.*) Page 50.

**long run, in the:** concerning a longer period in the future; in the end. Page 34.

**loot:** stolen money or valuables, often taken by violence or force. Page 92.

**lost sight of:** forgotten, disregarded or ignored. Page 60.

**lot: 1.** a large extent, amount or number, as in *"A lot of pleasure and happiness."* Page 23.
**2.** a number of persons or things regarded as a group, as in *"Men without faith are a pretty sorry lot."* Page 156.
**3.** one's fortune in life; fate, as in *"Oh, yes, it is true that such people, seeing one improve his lot, can become frantic and attack all the harder."* Page 198.

**low ebb:** in a bad state or condition. From the movement of the tide (the periodic rise and fall of the level of water in the ocean), with the *ebb* being the action of the water flowing away from the shore and going back out to sea. Page 162.

**low-income:** having a relatively small income or used by people on a relatively small income. *Low-income housing* would be housing for those on a small income and is often specifically developed and built with that public in mind, with financial assistance from the local or federal government. Page 80.

**low-mindedness:** the quality or characteristic of tending to think or behave in a hopeless, dispirited or discouraged manner. Page 111.

**lured:** tempted, attracted or persuaded (to do something or go somewhere) with the promise of pleasure. Page 112.

# M

**make nothing out of:** to treat with no respect or thoughtful concern; to have a low opinion of; value at a low rate. Page 195.

**malice:** a desire to harm others or to see others suffer. Page 50.

**malice aforethought:** legally, the intention to commit a wrongful act (such as murder) without just cause or excuse and which was determined upon before it was carried out. Page 53.

**mandate, heavenly:** a *mandate* is an authoritative command, instruction or order. A *heavenly mandate* would be a direction or command coming from a god. Page 168.

**map:** plan, sketch or draw out, especially in detail as if on a map, as in *"there is always a point on the road when one can map a new one."* Page 204.

**marketplace:** the world or sphere of business and trade where the buying and selling of goods or services takes place. Page 117.

**materialism:** any one of a family of metaphysical theories which view the universe as consisting of hard objects such as stones, big or very small. The theories seek to explain away such things as minds by saying they can be reduced to physical things or their motions. Materialism is a very ancient idea. There are other ideas. (From *author's footnote.*) Page 152.

**materialist:** one who believes in the doctrine of *materialism,* any one of a family of metaphysical theories which view the universe as consisting of hard objects such as stones, big or very small. The theories seek to explain away such things as minds by saying they can be reduced to physical things or their motions. Materialism is a very ancient idea. There are other ideas. Page 155.

**materialistic:** the opinion that only physical matter exists. (From *author's footnote.*) Page 30.

**measure:** extent, quantity or degree, as in *"one's survival and that of one's family and friends depends in no small measure upon the general competence of others."* Page 117.

**measures, strong:** procedures, laws, courses of action or plans (to achieve a particular purpose) that are forceful and effective. Page 72.

**mechanism:** the view that all life is only matter in motion and can be totally explained by physical laws. Advanced by Leucippus and Democritus (460 B.C. to 370 B.C.) who may have gotten it from Egyptian mythology. Upholders of this philosophy felt they had to neglect religion because they could not reduce it to mathematics. They were attacked by religious interests and in their turn attacked religions. Robert Boyle (1627–1691), who developed Boyle's Law in physics, refuted it by raising the question as to whether or not nature might have designs such as matter in motion. (From *author's footnote.*) Page 152.

**mechanisms:** the means by which something (mental or physical) is accomplished, likened to the structure or system of parts in a mechanical device for carrying out some function or doing something. Page 104.

**mechanist:** one who believes in the doctrine of *mechanism,* the view that all life is only matter in motion and can be totally explained by physical laws. *See also* **mechanism.** Page 155.

**medicinal:** of or relating to the properties of a medicine; intended to improve somebody's physical well-being. Page 20.

**menace:** something that threatens to cause evil, harm, injury, etc. Page 196.

**mercy of, at the:** without any protection against; entirely in the power of, or helpless before. Page 54.

**metaphysical:** of or relating to *metaphysics,* a branch of speculative inquiry or investigation, whose ideas or concepts are not verifiable by logical methods. *Speculative* means of a conclusion, an opinion, or a theory reached by guess or unfounded theory. The term, *metaphysical,* was first applied to writings of Aristotle (384–322 B.C.), and literally means "after physics," as these writings were placed by his editors after his books about nature, time, place, etc., known as the *Physics.* Page 152.

**might:** the power, force, authority or collective resources held and used by a group or government. Page 60.

**mischance:** the occurrence of unfortunate events by chance or bad luck; misfortune. Page 64.

**moral:** able to know right from wrong in conduct; deciding and acting from that understanding. (From *author's footnote.*) Page 30.

**morale:** the mental and emotional attitude of an individual or a group; sense of well-being; willingness to get on with it; a sense of common purpose. (From *author's footnote.*) Page 77.

**muddle:** a confused or disordered mental state. Page 122.

**murder:** the unlawful killing of one (or more) human being by another, especially with malice aforethought (intending to do so before the act). (From *author's footnote.*) Page 53.

**mutual agreement:** agreement shared between two or more persons, groups, countries, etc. *Mutual* means possessed in common; of or pertaining to each of two or more; shared. Page 40.

**mutually:** done or experienced equally by two or more people. Page 106.

**Napoleon:** Napoleon Bonaparte (1767–1821), French military leader who rose to power in France by military force, declared himself emperor and conducted campaigns of conquest across Europe until his final defeat in 1821 when he died from poison administered by one of his close associates. Page 186.

**no matter:** regardless of; it being of no importance. Page 26.

**novel:** of a new kind; different from anything seen or known before. Page 103.

**nurture:** to support and encourage, as during a period of training or development. Page 132.

**obligation: 1.** the condition or fact of owing another something in return for things, favors or services received. (From *author's footnote.*) Page 34.
**2.** the state, fact or condition of being indebted to another

for a special service or favor received; a duty, contract, promise or any other social, moral or legal requirement that binds one to follow or avoid a certain course of action; the sense of owing another. (From *author's footnote.*) Page 103.

**officers:** members of the armed forces who are in a position of authority over soldiers and who hold a *commission,* a document granting authority to military officers issued by the president of the United States. Page 86.

**off the rails:** out of the correct, normal or usual condition; not functioning, working or acting correctly. The phrase alludes to a train that has run off the railway tracks and is literally off its rails. Page 136.

**on the other hand:** used to indicate two contrasting sides of a subject; in contrast, oppositely. Page 64.

**open, in the:** not hidden or secret; so as to be seen. Page 184.

**opened the door:** created an opportunity for; provided the means of getting or reaching something. Page 162.

**opinion leaders:** the persons in a group to whom others listen, whose opinion they accept, whom they trust and on whom they depend. Page 67.

**out from underfoot:** no longer constantly (and annoyingly) present and in one's way or hindering one's progress, likened to something being under one's foot. Page 132.

**parrots:** persons who merely repeat the words or imitate the actions of another, especially without understanding them. *Parrot* is the tropical bird that has the ability to mimic human speech or other sounds. Page 132.

**party to:** to be involved in an agreement or action such as participating in or aiding another in a crime. Page 59.

**perjury:** the deliberate giving of false, misleading or incomplete data while under oath, such as in a court of law. Page 50.

**personify:** to be a symbol or perfect example of (some idea, thing, etc.). Page 136.

**phenomenon:** an observable fact or event. (From *author's footnote.*) Page 184.

**physics:** the science that deals with matter, energy, motion and force, including what these things are, why they behave as they do and the relationship between them, as contrasted to the life sciences, such as biology which studies and observes living organisms like animals and plants. Page 152.

**pieces, go to:** become upset or nervous to the extent that one cannot live, work or perform as one should; to be ruined or wrecked, likened to something breaking up into fragments. Page 86.

**pilloried:** exposed to ridicule, public contempt, scorn or abuse. (From *author's footnote.*) Page 58.

**plain:** absolute or total (used for emphasis). Page 124.

**Plato:** (427–347 B.C.) Greek philosopher noted for his works on law, mathematics, technical philosophic problems and natural science. In about 387 B.C., near Athens, Plato founded the most influential school of the ancient world, the Academy, where he taught until his death. His most famous pupil there was Aristotle. Page 159.

**plunges:** falls or gets thrown suddenly and uncontrollably (downward). Page 203.

**policies:** any governing principles, plans or courses of action. Page 88.

**political:** of or having to do with *politics,* the science or practice of government; the regulation and management of a nation or state for the preservation of its safety, peace and prosperity. *Government* is that controlling body of a nation, state or people which conducts its policy, actions and affairs. Page 60.

**practice:** to exercise or perform repeatedly in order to acquire or polish a skill. (From *author's footnote.*) Page 140.

**precautions:** actions taken in advance to prevent something dangerous, unpleasant, inconvenient, etc., from happening. Page 13.

**precepts:** rules or statements advising or laying down a principle or principles or a course of action regarding conduct; directions meant as a rule or rules for conduct. (From *author's footnote.*) Page 34.

**pretenses:** false appearances or actions intended to deceive; false displays of attitude, knowledge, etc. Page 120.

**prevalent:** widespread in existence or occurrence; widely or commonly occurring, existing, accepted or practiced. Page 26.

**priests:** persons who are trained and have the authority to perform religious duties and ceremonies in certain churches. *"Priests of old"* refers to such persons in past times, who, firmly convinced that they alone knew the truth about the world and religion, enforced their beliefs on others. Page 155.

**private sector, the:** the part of the economy of a country that is made up of companies and organizations that are not owned or controlled by the government. Page 69.

**probes, space:** unmanned spacecrafts designed to explore outer space and transmit data back to Earth. Page 82.

**production:** the act of completing something; finishing a task, project or object that is useful or valuable or simply worth doing or having. (From *author's footnote*.) Page 112.

**promiscuous:** casual, random sexual relations. (From *author's footnote*.) Page 23.

**propaganda:** spreading ideas, information or rumor to further one's own cause and/or injure that of another, often without regard to truth; the act of putting lies in the press or on radio and TV so that when a person comes to trial he will be found guilty; the action of falsely damaging a person's reputation so he will not be listened to. (A propagandist is a person or group that does, makes or practices propaganda.) (From *author's footnote*.) Page 58.

**propagandist:** *see* **propaganda**.

**propitiation:** the act of trying to please or satisfy someone (such as in making an offering or sacrifice) in a way calculated to win their favor in order to defend or protect oneself against their disapproval, attack, etc. Page 118.

**prosper:** to achieve economic success; succeeding at what one does. (From *author's footnote*.) Page 195.

**public workers:** those employed by the government on activities intended for the benefit or use of the general public, such as in schools, public hospitals, public transportation systems, construction projects and the like. Page 69.

# R

**rails, off the:** out of the correct, normal or usual condition; not functioning, working or acting correctly. The phrase alludes to a train that has run off the railway tracks and is literally off its rails. Page 136.

**rationalizations:** attempts to explain behavior normally considered irrational or unacceptable by offering apparently reasonable or sensible explanations. Page 104.

**read up on:** to learn about by reading; gather information on; research by reading. Page 66.

**recommendation(s):** something, such as a course of action, that is advised or suggested as appropriate, beneficial or the like. Page 43.

**reconcile:** resolve or end a conflict; solve or settle a quarrel or dispute. Page 40.

**refinement:** elegance of feeling, taste, manners, language, etc. Page 186.

**relief:** goods or money given by a government agency to people because of need or poverty. (From *author's footnote.*) Page 111.

**repress:** to keep down or under by self-control or suppression (of desires, feelings, actions, etc.); prevent from expression. Page 34.

**reveled in:** took great pleasure, delight or satisfaction in. Page 134.

**revered:** felt deep respect or admiration for (something). Page 167.

**revolution:** overthrow of a government, a form of government or a social system by those governed and usually by forceful or violent means, with another government or system taking its place. Page 134.

**-ridden:** used in combination with another word (placed at the end) meaning full of, burdened with, as in *"crime-ridden."* Page 57.

**right and left:** from all directions; on every side. Page 186.

**ripen:** come (or improve) to a state or condition of full or maximum development. Page 30.

**ritual dances:** a set, ordered and ceremonial way of performing dances, often carried out by primitive societies as part of religious custom, as in *"ritual dances before the hunt." Ritual* means the performance of actions or procedures (such as by formal custom, belief, etc.) in a very set and ordered manner. Page 118.

**roadbed:** literally, the foundation of soil or crushed rock that supports a road or highway. Hence, the underlying support or foundation along or upon which something can advance. Page 88.

**rule out:** exclude something as a possibility. Page 53.

**run its course:** complete its natural development without interference. *Course* in this sense means the continuous passage or progress through a succession of stages. Page 103.

# S

**safeguard:** prevent from being harmed; protect. (From *author's footnote.*) Page 75.

**saint(s):** somebody who has been particularly holy in life and after death is declared by a Christian church to have a privileged place in heaven and be worthy of worship. Also, someone who is a particularly good or holy person, or one who is extremely kind and patient in dealing with difficult people or situations. Page 160.

**scratch, from:** from a position of no previous advantage or knowledge; from nothing. A *scratch* is a line or mark drawn as an indication of a starting point in some sporting contest. Page 146.

**sea:** something that suggests the ocean in its extremely large or overpowering vastness; an overwhelming quantity, as in *"In this sea of contention, one bright principle has emerged: the right to believe as one chooses."* Page 154.

**self-reliant:** dependent on one's own efforts, capabilities, judgment or resources. Page 33.

**Seneca:** (4 B.C.–A.D. 65) Roman philosopher, playwright and statesman, who was one of the most renowned writers of Latin literature. He wrote numerous philosophical essays and plays, drawing moral lessons and attacking luxury and immorality. Page 159.

**serpent:** a snake, a legless animal with a long, thin, flexible body covered with overlapping scales that often has a poisonous bite. The term is usually applied to the larger, more poisonous snakes. Page 53.

**serve their own ends:** promote or advance their own intentions or desires to the exclusion of others. *Serve* means to be of assistance to or promote the interests of, and *ends* means the things an individual or group has for goals or intends to achieve. Page 44.

**serve their own purposes:** promote or advance their own intended or desired results without regard for others. *Serve* means to be of assistance to or promote the interests of, and *purposes* means the objects toward which one works or wishes to achieve. Page 124.

**set the stage for:** to prepare the way for or to make something likely; to provide the underlying basis or background for something to occur. This expression is from arranging actors and objects on a theatrical stage prior to the beginning of a play or an act in a play. Page 144.

**shadowed:** to become clouded over as if with shadows; grow dark or gloomy. Page 67.

**shalt, thou:** an old form of *you shall,* normally used in formal writing. Page 53.

**shatter:** break apart; disintegrate. Literally, *shatter* means to break into pieces as by a single blow. Page 26.

**shift (his) mental gears:** change one's ideas, conceptual approach, etc., in handling something such as a problem or situation. The phrase refers to the gears of an automobile which the driver shifts depending upon the speed required due to conditions such as hills, traffic, etc. Page 144.

**shortcomings:** faults or failures to meet a certain standard, typically in a person's character or conduct. Page 174.

**shut off (from):** put into a state of separation or isolation from. Page 100.

**slop over:** to spill over a boundary, typically as a result of careless handling and likened to water spilling over the edge of a container. Page 78.

**smooth the way:** to remove obstructions, hindrances or difficulties from a course or path. Page 67.

**smother:** to give someone too much emotion, affection, love, etc., so as to restrict, suppress or prevent expression. Page 32.

**solemnity:** the state or character of being deeply serious; lack of joy or humor. Page 187.

**sorry:** in a poor or pitiful state or condition; worthless or of little value. Page 156.

**sows:** causes some (negative) feeling or belief to arise or become widespread. Literally, *sow* means to plant the seeds of a plant or crop. Page 91.

**space probes:** unmanned spacecrafts designed to explore outer space and transmit data back to Earth. Page 82.

**special interest group:** a group of people or an organization seeking or receiving special advantages or treatment, typically through persuading political representatives or influential persons to issue laws in their favor. Page 64.

**species, dawn of the:** the first appearance or beginning of Mankind on Earth. *Dawn* means the beginning (of something) or the initial stage of a developmental process and *species* is the human race. Page 155.

**species, the:** the human race, Mankind. A *species* is a group or class of animals or plants having certain common and permanent characteristics which clearly distinguish it from other groups and which can breed with one another. Page 155.

**spite of, in:** regardless of; without being affected by the particular factor mentioned. Page 41.

**sportsmanship:** appropriate conduct according to principles of fairness, observation of rules, respect for others, good temper in losing, etc. Page 170.

**startles one half out of (his) wits:** frightens one extremely; *startle* means to alarm, frighten or surprise suddenly, and *wits* means one's mental composure or ability to think. Page 190.

**state:** the government of a country. Page 58.

**stockbroker:** one that acts as an agent in the buying and selling of stocks. (To raise money, companies, corporations, etc., sell *shares,* equal parts into which a company is divided and sold. *Stocks* are shares that someone has bought in a company. If the company does well the monetary value of the shares or stock goes up. If it does poorly, the monetary value of the shares or stock goes down.) Page 144.

**strain(s):** a specific variety of a disease that has unique characteristics, and which sometimes can develop resistance to treatments that were earlier successful in controlling the original version of the disease. Page 24.

**streak:** an element of a person's character, especially one that is only occasionally evident or that contrasts with other characteristics. (A *streak* is a line, mark, smear or band differentiated by color or texture from its surroundings.) Page 94.

**strings (attached):** conditions, limits or restrictions attached to something, such as an agreement, relationship, etc. Page 78.

**strong measures:** procedures, laws, courses of action or plans (to achieve a particular purpose) that are forceful and effective. Page 72.

**stuntmen:** those men who substitute for actors in scenes involving physical risk. Page 140.

**subterfuges:** secret, usually dishonest, ways of behaving or doing something; actions designed to hide, avoid or escape something. Page 39.

**suit their own ends:** satisfy or please their own intentions or desires (to the exclusion of others). *Suit* means satisfy, please or agree with the views or wishes of, and *ends* means the things an individual or group has for goals or intends to achieve. Page 48.

**sulfuric acid:** a highly corrosive, oily liquid that is used in batteries and in the manufacture of many products such as explosives, detergents, dyes and chemicals. Burning coal (used in many production facilities) produces a mist of sulfuric acid in the air, which turns rain into acid rain, causing harm to plants and fish, corrosion of metals, and deterioration of stone and other building materials. Page 82.

**survival:** the act of remaining alive, of continuing to exist, of being alive. (From *author's footnote.*) Page 5.

**tailor-made:** made or adapted for a particular purpose. From the idea of clothes that are "tailor-made" (made by a tailor) rather than in a factory. Page 34.

**take(s): 1.** to perform, make or do (an act, action, movement, etc.), as in *"Insist when someone is ill that he or she takes the proper precautions and gets proper care."* Page 13.
**2.** receive something into the body, as by swallowing; consume, as in *"Do not take harmful drugs."* Page 19.
**3.** to end (a life), as in *"Drinking can take lives in more ways than one."* Page 20.
**4.** to obtain or determine, as through measurement or a specified procedure, as in *"take the temperatures."* Page 70.
**5.** (of a task or situation) needs or calls for; requires, as in *"It might take a while."* Page 190.

**take a hand in:** participate or be involved in, as in *"Aside from personal benefit, one can take a hand, no matter how small, in beginning a new era for human relations."* Page 191.

**take care of:** to assume responsibility for the support, treatment or maintenance of; see to the safety or well-being of, as in *"Take care of yourself."* Page 13.

**taken: 1.** performed, made or done (an act, action, movement, etc.), as in *"strong measures should be advocated and taken to defend them and keep them from harm."* Page 72.
**2.** required, as in *"yet it has taken a violent revolution to handle them."* Page 134.
**3.** experienced or felt, as in *"Man, since the dawn of the species, has taken great consolation and joy in his religions."* Page 155.

**taken away:** removed from someone's possession, as in *"taken away from them by brothers, sisters or parents."* Page 78.

**take over:** to assume management, control of or responsibility for, as in *"be readied to take over tomorrow's world."* Page 132.

**take refuge in:** turn to something as a means of escape, comfort or the like, as in *"When one is weak, it is a temptation to take refuge in subterfuges and lies."* Page 39.

**tangible:** real or actual, rather than imaginary or visionary. Literally, capable of being touched or felt. Page 114.

**tattered:** torn and ragged. Page 203.

**tedious:** tiresome or boring because of being long, dull or repetitive. Page 168.

**temperate:** not going to extremes; not overdoing things; controlling one's cravings. (From *author's footnote.*) Page 19.

**terrain:** an area of land, seen in terms of its surface features or general physical character. Page 84.

**thou shalt:** an old form of *you shall,* normally used in formal writing. Page 53.

**time and place, in its own:** during that specified time period and location. The use of *own* emphasizes the idea of a specific environment and time (in this case, the late 1700s and early 1800s in the United States, France and South America). Page 60.

**tomes:** books, especially large heavy (sometimes old) books on serious subjects. Page 168.

**trash bin of incompetence:** figuratively, a place where inability, lack of skill or ineffectiveness are dumped and stored. From *trash bin* meaning a container where refuse, garbage, unwanted or worthless material or objects are disposed of. Page 126.

**treacherous:** marked by unforeseen hazards; dangerous or deceptive. Page 130.

**trial and error:** the process of making repeated trials or tests, improving the methods used based on the errors made, until the right result is found. Page 138.

**truth:** that which agrees with the facts and observations; logical answers resulting from looking over all the facts and data; a conclusion based on evidence uninfluenced by desire, authority or prejudice; an inevitable (unavoidable) fact no matter how arrived at. (From *author's footnote.*) Page 47.

**turns:** changes or developments in a particular direction. Page 144.

**tyrannical:** the use of cruel, unjust and absolute power; crushing; oppressing; harsh; severe. (From *author's footnote.*) Page 60.

**tyrannical days of aristocracy:** a reference to Europe of the 1500s, 1600s and 1700s when countries were ruled by kings holding complete power. Under the kings were the aristocrats, born to great wealth and holding far greater rights and privileges than the rest of the population. It was against this background that revolutions occurred in the late 1700s and early 1800s in the United States (against the rule of Britain), France (against the rule of the French King and the aristocrats) and in South America (against the rule of Spain). Page 60.

**tyranny:** a government in which a single ruler has absolute power and uses it unjustly or cruelly. Page 67.

**unavailing:** unsuccessful or ineffective; of no use; producing no result. Page 118.

**underfoot, out from:** no longer constantly (and annoyingly) present and in one's way or hindering one's progress, likened to something being under one's foot. Page 132.

**unkempt:** having an untidy or disorderly appearance; uncared-for or neglected. Page 77.

**unlooked-for:** not anticipated; unexpected; not hoped for. Page 106.

**unscrupulous:** not restrained by moral or ethical principles. Page 63.

**untimely:** occurring or done at a bad time. Page 64.

**unwittingly:** unknowingly; unconsciously; without awareness. Page 106.

**up in the world, got:** became more important, successful or prosperous in society. Page 196.

**usurp:** to seize and hold (the power or rights of another, for example) by force and in an unjust or illegal manner. Page 63.

# V

**vandalism:** the willful and malicious destruction of public or private property, especially anything beautiful or artistic. (From *author's footnote.*) Page 78.

**verge: 1.** either of the two edges or borders along a road, usually unpaved, as in *"the motorist who plunges off onto the verge."* Page 203.
**2.** the extreme edge of something such as an extreme limit beyond which something specified will happen, as in *"seek by various means to push one onto the verge."* Page 204.

**virtues:** the ideal qualities in good human conduct. (From *author's footnote.*) Page 167.

**waived aside:** put aside or dismissed from consideration or discussion. Page 160.

**way, a little (something) goes a long:** a small amount of something can have a great effect or a strong influence with (a person). Page 20.

**will:** bearing or attitude toward others; disposition. Traditionally, "men of good will" means those who mean well toward their fellows and work to help them. (From *author's footnote.*) Page 69.

**wind of mischance:** an unlucky force or influence. *Wind* in this sense means a force, influence or tendency that drives or carries something along, or to which one is exposed, and *mischance* means the occurrence of unfortunate events by chance or bad luck; misfortune. Page 64.

**wind up:** to arrive in a situation after or because of a course of action; end up. Page 20.

**witness, bear false:** to tell lies or state something false while under oath or in a court of law; to state falsely. *Bear* means to give or provide. *Witness* means swearing to a fact, statement, etc.; proof or evidence. Page 50.

**wits:** mind; powers of thinking and reasoning. Page 120.

**wits, startles one half out of (his):** frightens one extremely; *startle* means to alarm, frighten or surprise suddenly, and *wits* means one's mental composure or ability to think. Page 190.

**wretched:** extremely bad or unpleasant, miserable. Page 92.

**wringing wet:** very wet; so wet that liquid may be extracted by or as if by twisting or squeezing (wringing). Page 76.

*Z*

**zealots:** people who show excessive enthusiasm for and devotion to some cause, belief or subject and determinedly try to advance it; fanatics. Page 152.

*All you have to do is keep*
*The Way to Happiness flowing in the society.*
*Like gentle oil spread upon the raging sea,*
*the calm will flow outward and outward.*

The conduct and actions of others
affects your own survival.

The Way to Happiness includes
helping your contacts and friends.

Begin with close friends and
contacts that affect your survival.
Give them *The Way to Happiness*
and several additional copies—so they too
can spread the calm outward and outward.

This book is also available in
pocket-size booklets in quantities of 12.

Special discounts exist for schools,
civic groups, government organizations and businesses
as well as other programs allowing for
individuals and groups to republish this book
for widespread distribution.

For more information contact
The Way to Happiness Foundation:
**www.thewaytohappiness.org**